D1333113

the potato cookbook

recipes featuring the world's greatest vegetable

recipes featuring the world's greatest vegetable

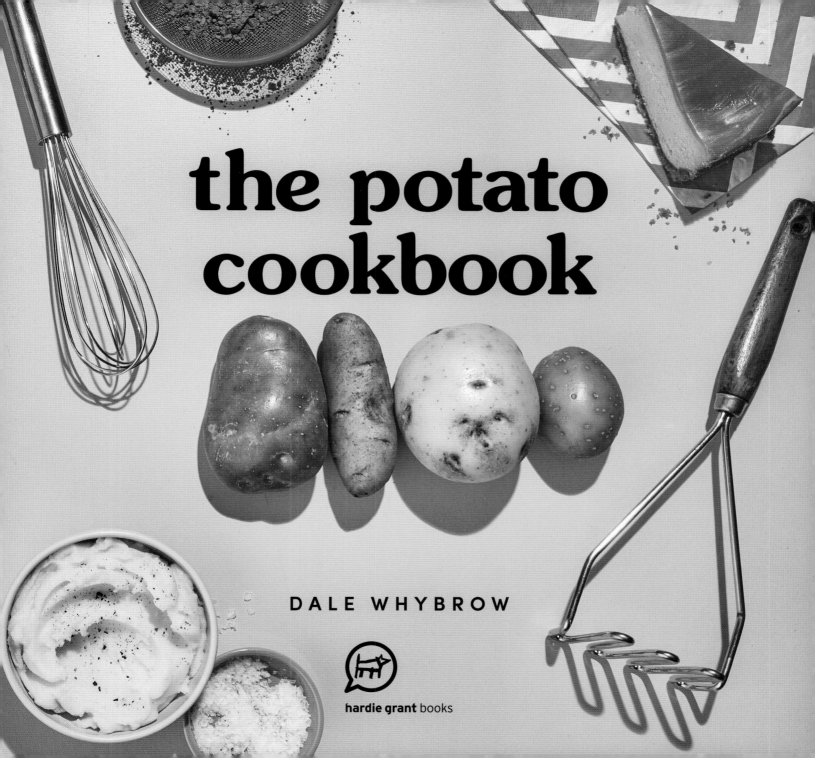

the potato
cookbook

DALE WHYBROW

hardie grant books

To my dear parents, Dawn and Leo, who taught me that
it's always worth making the extra effort.

contents

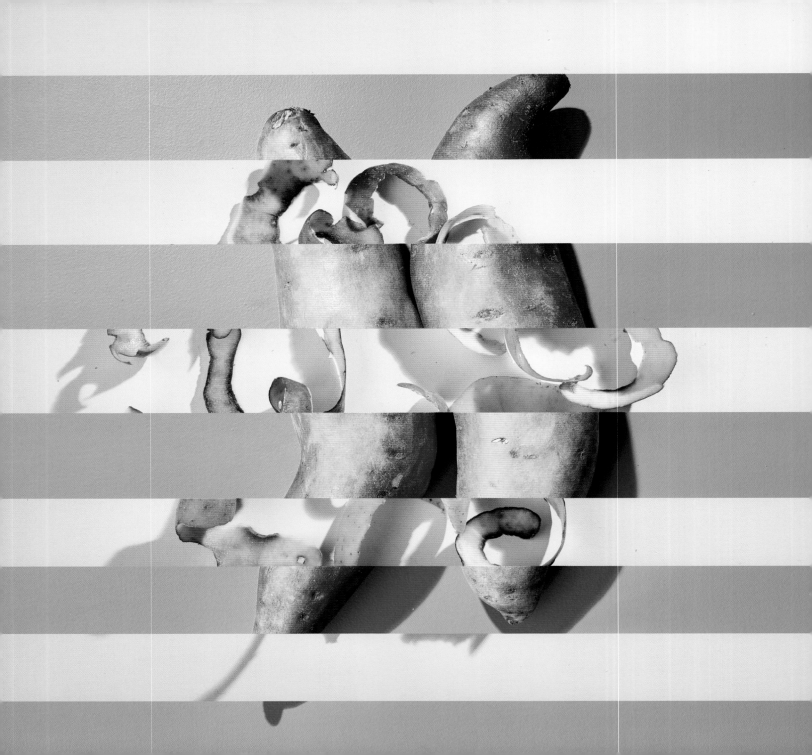

introduce

Everybody loves potatoes. And what's not to love? This humble and widely available vegetable is just as delicious soft and buttery in a mash, crispy and sprinkled with salt, cold and refreshing in a salad, or even moist and dense in a chocolate cake.

At my table, barely a day goes by without potatoes making an appearance. If it's a celebration, potatoes will have a starring role, no question. If it's a weeknight dinner, they usually make an appearance, too. There's always a bit of jostling and elbowing to be the person with the best access to the potato dish of the day. And leftovers – they're called second helpings.

When I first started cooking with potatoes, I made classics like potato bake, potato salad and potato soup – staples I still whip up today. But while exploring an American supermarket a couple of years ago, I discovered potato chips coated in chocolate. What a revelation! I was hooked, and I soon made my first batch of cookies mixing rich chocolate and salty potato chips. Then I made chocolate and potato chip bark. Then I started thinking what else I could make with potato … and I haven't stopped since!

This book is my celebration of the potato dishes we know and love, plus recipes that use potatoes in ways you may not have thought of before: in ice creams, in breads, in cakes, even in healthy crackers. They're all delicious. I hope this book starts you thinking about the different ways you can cook with potatoes, and that you love these recipes as much as my family and friends do.

Dale Whybrow

choose

Potatoes fall into three general categories – floury (or roasting), waxy or all-purpose potatoes – which define their basic characteristics and also the best ways to cook with them. Choosing the best potato for your recipe will have a big impact on the success of your dish.

FLOURY (OR ROASTING) POTATOES

(also known as starchy potatoes, high-starch potatoes or fluffy potatoes)

VARIETIES

- COLIBAN
- RUSSET
- IDAHO
- SUPERIOR
- VIVALDI
- KATAHDIN
- KING EDWARD
- ROOSTER
- MARIS PIPER
- KESTREL
- BISON
- EUREKA
- ESTIMA
- MARABEL

GOOD FOR

Use floury potatoes for the best mash, fries, wedges, chips (crisps), smooth soups, gnocchi, whole baked potatoes in their skins, and roast potato pieces coated in fat or oil. These are also the ones to choose for breads, cakes or slices where the recipe calls for mashed potato.

WAXY POTATOES

(also known as low-starch potatoes)

———— VARIETIES ————

- KIPFLER
- RED BLISS
- HUCKLEBERRY
- NEW (BABY)
- CHARLOTTE
- MARIS PEER
- RUSSIAN
  BANANA
- PINK FIR
  APPLE
- PURPLE
  VIKING
- JERSEY ROYAL
- NADINE
- ANYA
- FINGERLING
- NICOLA
- PATRONE
- PINK EYE
- PURPLE
  CONGO
- CAROLA

———— GOOD FOR ————

Use waxy potatoes for the best salads, chunky soups, potato bakes, stews and gratins. They're also great for breads that include cubes of potato.

ALL-PURPOSE POTATOES

(also known as medium-starch potatoes)

———— VARIETIES ————

- DUTCH
  CREAM
- YUKON GOLD
- KENNEBEC
- SPUNTA
- MOONLIGHT
- BINTJE
- YELLOW FINN
- OSPREY
- RED GOLD
- NORLAND RED
- ROYAL BLUE
- OTWAY RED
- DESIREE
- TOOLANGI
  DELIGHT
- KENNEBEC
- PURPLE
  PERUVIAN
- GOLDEN
  DELIGHT
- SEBAGO
- PONTIAC
- RED RASCAL

———— GOOD FOR ————

Use as per floury or waxy potatoes.

boil & simmer

potato, corn and tuna chowder

This is a much-loved recipe in my family. We like it served with crusty bread and lots of butter. We like it served often. Some of us like extra cheese stirred into our serving, while others like to dunk their bread. Whichever way you have it, this is a delicious soup and perfect for winter gatherings.

Use waxy potatoes; see pages 002–003 for a list of varieties.

1 tablespoon olive oil

2 medium onions, finely diced

3 celery stalks, sliced

1 red capsicum (bell pepper), seeded and diced

1 litre (34 fl oz/4 cups) chicken stock (low-salt)

3 medium potatoes, about 500 g (1 lb 2 oz), peeled and cut into 1 cm (½ in) cubes

2 large carrots, halved lengthways and sliced

2 large zucchini (courgettes), halved lengthways and sliced

corn kernels, sliced from 2 corn cobs

½ teaspoon sea salt

½ teaspoon freshly ground black pepper, plus extra to serve

850 g (1 lb 14 oz) tinned tuna in olive oil

75 g (2¾ oz/½ cup) plain (all-purpose) flour

1 litre (34 fl oz/4 cups) full-cream (whole) milk

10 g (¼ oz/⅓ cup) chopped fresh flat-leaf (Italian) parsley

60 g (2 oz/½ cup) grated cheddar cheese, or more to taste

1. Heat the olive oil in a large saucepan over medium heat and cook the onions, celery and capsicum until softened, stirring occasionally, about 10 minutes. Add the stock, potatoes, carrots, zucchini, corn, sea salt and pepper and bring to the boil. Cover with a lid and reduce the heat to medium–low. Simmer the chowder until the vegetables are tender, about 30 minutes.

2. Drain the tuna, put it in a medium mixing bowl and flake with a fork.

3. In a medium mixing bowl, whisk the flour and 125 ml (4 fl oz/½ cup) of milk together until smooth. Add a further 125 ml of milk and whisk again until smooth.

4. Add the milk and flour mixture to the chowder with the remainder of the milk, the flaked tuna and half of the chopped parsley and bring to the boil over medium–high heat, stirring often. Reduce the heat to medium–low and simmer for 5 minutes, stirring occasionally. Taste and add more salt and pepper if needed.

5. Serve in individual bowls, garnished with the remaining chopped parsley, pepper and grated cheese.

sweet potato, fennel and ginger soup with spiced pears

Sweet potato is delicious when teamed with fennel and ginger in this perfect autumn soup – and with the spiced pears it's really something special.

Use orange sweet potatoes.

for the soup

1 tablespoon olive oil

1 large onion, diced

1 fennel bulb, trimmed, cored and diced

2 celery stalks, sliced

1 large carrot, halved lengthways and sliced

2 garlic cloves, sliced

2 teaspoons grated fresh ginger

1.5 litres (51 fl oz/6 cups) vegetable stock
 (low-salt)

2 medium–large sweet potatoes, about 900 g
 (2 lb), peeled and cut into 3 cm (1¼ in) pieces

½ teaspoon sea salt

for the spiced pears

2 just ripe pears, peeled, cored and quartered

1 tablespoon honey

2 thin strips of orange rind, about 8 cm (3¼ in)
 long

1 star anise

1 teaspoon lemon juice

½ teaspoon ground cinnamon

to serve

fresh thyme leaves

freshly ground black pepper

1. To make the soup, heat the olive oil in a large saucepan over medium heat and cook the onion, fennel, celery and carrot until soft, stirring occasionally, about 10 minutes. Add the garlic and ginger and cook until fragrant, about 2 minutes. Add the stock, sweet potatoes and sea salt and bring to the boil. Reduce the heat to medium–low and simmer until all the vegetables are tender, about 20 minutes.

2. Meanwhile, to make the spiced pears, combine 250 ml (8½ fl oz/1 cup) water with the pears, honey, orange rind, star anise, lemon juice and cinnamon in a small saucepan and bring to the boil over medium–high heat. Reduce the heat to medium–low and simmer until the pears are tender, about 10–15 minutes. Drain the pears, reserving the cooking water and discarding the orange rind and star anise. Slice each pear quarter into 3 slices.

3. Take the soup off the heat and blend with a hand-held blender until smooth. Stir in 60 ml (2 fl oz/¼ cup) of the reserved pear cooking water, adding more if required until it reaches your preferred consistency. Return the soup to medium heat and stir until bubbling.

4. Serve in individual bowls, garnished with pear slices and sprinkled with thyme and pepper.

sweet potato, ginger and miso soup

This soup is as nourishing as it sounds, and completely delicious. Miso, the savoury paste made from fermented soybeans, is the perfect balance for the sweet potato. For the meat eaters, some shredded cooked chicken added to the individual serving bowls makes a tasty addition.

Use orange sweet potatoes.

1 tablespoon olive oil

1 medium onion, diced

1 celery stalk, sliced

1 large carrot, halved lengthways and sliced

2 garlic cloves, sliced

2 teaspoons grated fresh ginger

1.5 litres (51 fl oz/6 cups) vegetable stock (low-salt)

1 large sweet potato, about 650 g (1 lb 7 oz), peeled and chopped

2 medium zucchini (courgettes), halved lengthways and sliced

2 tablespoons white (shiro) miso paste

2 teaspoons soy sauce

to serve

2 teaspoons sliced fresh chives

1 teaspoon sesame oil

1. Heat the olive oil in a large saucepan over medium heat and cook the onion, celery and carrot until soft, stirring occasionally, about 10 minutes. Stir in the garlic and ginger and cook until fragrant, about 2 minutes. Add the stock, sweet potato and zucchini and bring to the boil. Reduce the heat to medium–low and simmer until the vegetables are tender, about 20 minutes.

2. Take the soup off the heat and blend with a hand-held blender until smooth. Return to medium heat until bubbling. Remove the soup from the heat.

3. Whisk the miso paste with 80 ml (2½ fl oz/ ⅓ cup) of water until smooth and stir through the soup with the soy sauce.

4. Serve in individual bowls, sprinkled with chives and a dribble of sesame oil.

potato and celeriac soup

Celeriac, part of the celery family, has a mellow flavour that works really well with potato. Combined with cumin and coriander, they make a beautiful winter soup.

Use floury (starchy or roasting) potatoes; see pages 002–003 for a list of varieties.

1 tablespoon olive oil

1 large onion, diced

2 large garlic cloves, sliced

½ teaspoon ground cumin

½ teaspoon ground coriander

1 medium celeriac, about 500 g (1 lb 2 oz), peeled and chopped

4 medium potatoes, about 600 g (1 lb 5 oz), peeled and chopped

1 litre (34 fl oz/4 cups) chicken stock (low-salt)

½ teaspoon sea salt

to serve

90 g (3 oz/⅓ cup) sour cream or Greek yoghurt

30 g (1 oz/¼ cup) chopped walnuts or pecans

1 tablespoon finely chopped fresh flat-leaf (Italian) parsley

freshly ground black pepper

1. Preheat the oven to 170°C (340°F) and line a baking tray with baking paper.

2. Heat the olive oil in a large saucepan over medium heat. Cook the onion, stirring, until it is softened but not browned, about 4 minutes. Add the garlic, cumin and coriander to the saucepan and stir for 2 minutes to release the aroma of the spices. Add the celeriac, potato, stock and sea salt to the saucepan and bring the soup to the boil. Reduce the heat to medium–low and simmer until the vegetables are tender, about 20 minutes.

3. While the soup is simmering, toast the walnuts. Spread the walnuts over the baking tray and toast in the oven until they are lightly golden and smell toasty, about 6 minutes.

4. Take the soup off the heat and blend with a hand-held blender until smooth. Return to medium heat until bubbling. Taste and add more sea salt if required.

5. To serve, ladle the soup into bowls. Garnish each bowl with sour cream and sprinkle with walnuts, parsley and pepper.

potato, leek and cashew soup

I love the classic combination of potatoes and leeks, which is taken to a new level of deliciousness with the addition of cashew cream. Your vegan and non-vegan friends alike will adore this soup, so it's a winner all round.

Use floury (starchy or roasting) potatoes; see pages 002–003 for a list of varieties.

for the cashew cream

115 g (4 oz/¾ cup) raw cashew nuts

1 tablespoon lemon juice

for the soup

1 tablespoon olive oil

1 small onion, finely chopped

2 leeks, white and pale green parts only, well rinsed and finely sliced

1 celery stalk, finely sliced

1 garlic clove, finely chopped

1 litre (34 fl oz/4 cups) vegetable stock (low-salt)

3 large potatoes, about 750 g (1 lb 11 oz), peeled and cut into 1.5 cm (½ in) cubes

1 bay leaf

½ teaspoon sea salt

¼ teaspoon freshly ground black pepper

to serve

1 tablespoon chopped fresh flat-leaf (Italian) parsley

1. To make the cashew cream, place the cashew nuts in a medium mixing bowl, cover with cold water and soak overnight. Drain and rinse the cashew nuts and add to a blender with 125 ml (4 fl oz/½ cup) of cold water and the lemon juice. Blend on a high setting until creamy, about 45 seconds.

2. To make the soup, heat the olive oil in a large saucepan over medium heat and cook the onion, leeks and celery until soft, stirring occasionally, about 10 minutes. Add the garlic and cook for a further 2 minutes. Pour in the stock and add the potatoes, bay leaf, sea salt and pepper. Increase the heat to medium–high and bring the soup to the boil, then reduce the heat to medium–low and simmer until the potatoes are tender, about 20 minutes.

3. Remove from the heat and discard the bay leaf. Using a potato masher, mash the potatoes into the soup until no large pieces remain or your desired consistency is achieved.

4. Return the soup to medium heat and stir in the cashew cream. Heat until bubbling, about 3 minutes. Taste and add more sea salt and pepper if needed.

5. Ladle the soup into bowls and garnish with a sprinkle of parsley.

pea, ham and potato soup

It's late Saturday afternoon and it's a wild, windy, winter's day. It's freezing cold – glove and scarf weather. A bowl of this will have you warm and cosy in no time. Some quick cheesy potato bread (page 134) on the side is perfect for dunking.

Use floury (starchy or roasting) potatoes; see pages 002–003 for a list of varieties.

for the stock

1 ham hock, about 1 kg (2 lb 3 oz)

1 medium onion, quartered

1 medium carrot, roughly chopped

1 celery stalk, roughly chopped

2 garlic cloves, peeled and left whole

2 bay leaves

10 black peppercorns

for the soup

30 g (1 oz) unsalted butter

1 medium onion, sliced

1 medium carrot, halved lengthways and sliced

2 celery stalks, sliced

1 garlic clove, finely sliced

3 medium potatoes, about 500 g (1 lb 2 oz), peeled and cut into 2 cm (¾ in) cubes

2 teaspoons fresh thyme leaves

½ teaspoon freshly ground black pepper

155 g (5½ oz/1 cup) frozen peas, or use fresh peas

to serve

1 tablespoon sliced fresh mint leaves

1. Put the ham hock in a large saucepan and cover with cold water. Bring to the boil over medium–high heat and boil for 5 minutes. Drain and rinse the ham hock and discard the cooking water. Rinse the saucepan.

2. To make the stock, return the ham hock to the saucepan and cover with cold water, at least 2 litres (68 fl oz/8 cups). Add the onion, carrot, celery, garlic, bay leaves and peppercorns. Bring to the boil over medium–high heat, then reduce the heat to medium–low and simmer until the ham hock is starting to fall apart, about 1½ hours. Remove the ham hock and set aside. Strain and set aside the cooking liquid (ham stock), discarding all the solids.

3. To make the soup, melt the butter in a large saucepan over medium heat and cook the onion until soft, about 5 minutes. Add the carrot, celery and garlic and cook, stirring occasionally, until soft, about 5 minutes. Add 1.25 litres (42 fl oz/5 cups) of ham stock, the potatoes, thyme and pepper. Bring to the boil and simmer until the potatoes are tender, about 20 minutes. Add the peas and simmer until the peas are cooked, about 2 minutes. Blend until semi-smooth using a hand-held blender or roughly mash with a potato masher.

4. Shred the meat from the ham hock and discard the skin and bone. Reserve ½ cup of shredded ham and stir the remaining ham into the soup. Taste the soup and add sea salt and more pepper if needed.

5. To serve, ladle the soup into individual bowls and top with the reserved shredded ham and mint leaves.

cauliflower and potato soup

The puréed potatoes and cauliflower make this soup so creamy there's no need to add any milk. The swirl of sour cream and the parmesan cheese on top add decadent richness, although they can be omitted if you're looking for a vegan option.

Use floury (starchy or roasting) potatoes; see pages 002–003 for a list of varieties.

1 tablespoon olive oil

1 onion, diced

2 celery stalks, sliced

1 garlic clove, finely chopped

1 litre (34 fl oz/4 cups) vegetable stock (low-salt)

3 medium potatoes, about 500 g (1 lb 2 oz), peeled and cut into 3 cm (1¼ in) pieces

½ small cauliflower, about 400 g (14 oz), trimmed and cut into 1.5 cm (½ in) pieces

2 bay leaves

½ teaspoon sea salt

¼ teaspoon freshly ground black pepper, plus extra to serve

to serve

60 g (2 oz/¼ cup) sour cream

25 g (1 oz/¼ cup) freshly grated parmesan cheese

1 tablespoon chopped fresh flat-leaf (Italian) parsley

1. Heat the olive oil in a large saucepan over medium heat and cook the onion and celery until softened, stirring occasionally, about 8 minutes. Add the garlic and cook for a further 2 minutes. Pour in the stock and add the potatoes, cauliflower, bay leaves, sea salt and pepper. Increase the heat to medium–high and bring the soup to the boil, then reduce the heat to medium–low and simmer until the potatoes and cauliflower are tender, about 20 minutes.

2. Remove from the heat and discard the bay leaves. Using a hand-held blender, purée the soup. Taste and add more sea salt and pepper if needed.

3. To serve, ladle the soup into bowls and garnish with sour cream, parmesan cheese, parsley and pepper.

potato, beer and smoked cheddar soup

Potatoes, beer and cheese. This might just be the best potato soup you've ever tasted. The beer gives an amazing depth of flavour to the potatoes, and cheese enhances almost anything. Serve with thick slices of buttered toast.

Use floury (starchy or roasting) potatoes; see pages 002–003 for a list of varieties.

1 tablespoon olive oil

150 g (5½ oz) rindless bacon rashers (slices), diced

1 large onion, diced

1 leek, white and pale green parts only, well rinsed and finely sliced

2 garlic cloves, finely chopped

2 celery stalks, sliced

375 ml (12½ fl oz/1½ cups) pale ale or other pale beer

1 litre (34 fl oz/4 cups) chicken stock (low-salt)

5 medium potatoes, about 900 g (2 lb), peeled and cut into 2 cm (¾ in) pieces

2 bay leaves

1 teaspoon worcestershire sauce

1 teaspoon dijon mustard

1 teaspoon fresh thyme leaves

¼ teaspoon sea salt

¼ teaspoon freshly ground black pepper

125 ml (4 fl oz/½ cup) thick (heavy) cream

120 g (4½ oz/1 cup) grated smoked cheddar cheese (or use plain cheddar cheese, or a combination)

to serve

2 tablespoons chopped fresh flat-leaf (Italian) parsley

1. Heat the olive oil in a large saucepan over medium heat and fry the bacon until crisp, about 5 minutes. Transfer the bacon to a plate lined with paper towel and set aside.

2. Add the onion, leek, garlic and celery to the saucepan and cook until softened, stirring occasionally, about 5 minutes. Increase the heat to medium–high and pour in the beer. Stir until bubbling, then add the stock, potatoes, bay leaves, worcestershire sauce, mustard, thyme, sea salt and pepper and bring to the boil. Reduce the heat to medium–low, cover and simmer until the potatoes are tender, about 20 minutes.

3. Take the soup off the heat and discard the bay leaves. Using a hand-held blender, purée the soup until completely smooth, or your desired consistency is achieved.

4. Return the soup to medium heat and add the cream and cheese. Stir until the cheese is completely melted. Taste and add more sea salt and pepper if needed.

5. To serve, ladle the soup into bowls and garnish with the reserved bacon and parsley.

curried chicken and potato soup

My family loves this warming winter soup, sweet and spicy from the curry powder. You'll love how easy it is to make, too. Everything gets thrown into the pot and simmers away while you get on with other things. A perfect weeknight dinner served with slices of buttermilk potato bread (page 135).

Use waxy potatoes; see pages 002–003 for a list of varieties.

1 tablespoon vegetable oil

1 large onion, diced

150 g (5½ oz) rindless bacon rashers (slices), diced

500 g (1 lb 2 oz) boneless, skinless chicken thigh fillets, chopped into 2 cm (¾ in) pieces

2 teaspoons curry powder

1 garlic clove, finely chopped

1.5 litres (51 fl oz/6 cups) chicken stock (low-salt)

3 medium–large potatoes, about 600 g (1 lb 5 oz), peeled and cut into 1 cm (½ in) cubes

1 large carrot, diced

corn kernels, sliced from 1 large corn cob

65 g (2¼ oz/⅓ cup) uncooked long-grain rice

½ teaspoon sea salt

¼ teaspoon dried thyme

¼ teaspoon dried marjoram or ¼ teaspoon extra dried thyme

¼ teaspoon freshly ground black pepper

to serve

2 tablespoons chopped fresh coriander (cilantro), or use fresh parsley if you prefer

1. Heat the vegetable oil in a large saucepan over medium–high heat and cook the onion and bacon, stirring, until they are starting to sizzle, about 3 minutes. Add the chicken and stir until the outside of the chicken no longer looks pink, about 4 minutes.

2. Add the curry powder and garlic and stir until fragrant, about 1 minute. Add the stock, potatoes, carrot, corn kernels, rice, sea salt, thyme, marjoram and pepper and bring to the boil. Reduce the heat to medium–low and simmer, covered, until the vegetables are tender and the rice is cooked, about 30 minutes.

3. Ladle the soup into bowls and garnish with chopped coriander or parsley.

weeknight chicken and potato curry

The combination of sweet and savoury spices in the curry powder makes this a winner with the whole family. If you want to ramp up the heat, add a sliced red chilli when you cook the garlic and ginger.

Use waxy potatoes; see pages 002–003 for a list of varieties.

2 tablespoons vegetable oil

800 g (1 lb 12 oz) boneless, skinless chicken thigh fillets, cut into 3 cm (1¼ in) pieces

1 large onion, sliced into thin wedges

2 garlic cloves, finely chopped

2 teaspoons finely chopped ginger

3 teaspoons curry powder

½ teaspoon ground cumin

½ teaspoon freshly ground black pepper

½ teaspoon sea salt

500 ml (17 fl oz/2 cups) chicken stock (low-salt)

400 g (14 oz) tinned chopped tomatoes

3 medium–large potatoes, about 600 g (1 lb 5 oz), peeled and cut into 1 cm (½ in) cubes

1 large carrot, halved lengthways and sliced

400 g (14 oz/2 cups) uncooked long-grain rice

90 g (3 oz/1½ cups) broccoli florets

250 ml (8½ fl oz/1 cup) coconut milk

2 tablespoons lemon juice

to serve

15 g (½ oz/¼ cup) chopped fresh coriander (cilantro)

1. Heat the vegetable oil in a large frying pan over medium–high heat. Add the chicken and stir until coloured on all sides, about 4 minutes. (You may need to do this in 2 batches, depending on the size of your frying pan.)

2. Add the onion wedges and cook until softened, stirring often, about 3 minutes. Reduce the heat to medium and stir in the garlic, ginger, curry powder, cumin, pepper and sea salt until the chicken is well coated and the spices are fragrant, about 2 minutes. Pour in the stock and the tomatoes and add the potatoes and carrot. Bring to the boil, then reduce the heat to medium–low and simmer until the vegetables are almost tender, about 15 minutes.

3. While the curry is simmering, cook the rice using your preferred method or the packet instructions.

4. Add the broccoli, coconut milk and lemon juice and simmer for 5 more minutes.

5. Serve in individual bowls, sprinkled with the coriander.

sweet potato macaroni cheese

The golden richness of sweet potato and the savoury flavour of Vegemite lift this macaroni cheese to the sublime. Add crisp breadcrumbs to the mix and this may well become your new favourite.

Use orange sweet potatoes.

2 medium sweet potatoes, about 600 g (1 lb 5 oz), peeled and cut into 4 cm (1½ in) pieces

1 teaspoon salt for the macaroni cooking water

300 g (10½ oz) macaroni

625 ml (21 fl oz/2½ cups) full-cream (whole) milk

1 tablespoon Vegemite, or use soy sauce

60 g (2 oz) unsalted butter

35 g (1¼ oz/¼ cup) plain (all-purpose) flour

½ teaspoon freshly ground black pepper

185 g (6½ oz/1½ cups) grated cheddar cheese

50 g (1¾ oz/½ cup) grated parmesan cheese

35 g (1¼ oz/⅓ cup) panko (Japanese-style) breadcrumbs

1. Preheat the oven to 180°C (350°F).

2. Put the sweet potatoes in a medium saucepan and cover with cold water. Bring to the boil over medium–high heat and boil until very tender, about 15 minutes, testing with the point of a sharp knife. Drain, reserving 250 ml (8½ fl oz/1 cup) of the cooking water, and return the sweet potatoes to the saucepan over low heat for 1 minute to ensure any excess water has evaporated. Mash thoroughly until very smooth.

3. To cook the macaroni, bring a large saucepan of salted water to the boil over high heat. When the water is boiling, add the macaroni and cook until still slightly firm, about 7–8 minutes. Drain and set aside.

4. Heat the milk and Vegemite in a saucepan over medium heat until almost boiling, whisking constantly to ensure the Vegemite dissolves in the milk.

5. In a separate saucepan over medium heat, melt the butter until foamy and add the flour, stirring until smooth. Stir over the heat for 2 minutes to cook out the floury taste. Remove from the heat and whisk in the hot Vegemite milk, a little at a time. Continue to whisk as you add more milk and the sauce thickens. When all the milk is added, put the sauce back over medium heat until bubbling. Add the pepper and cheddar cheese and stir until the cheese is melted. Stir in 125 ml (4 fl oz/½ cup) of the sweet potato cooking water until the sauce is smooth and creamy.

Recipe continues on next page.

sweet potato
macaroni cheese (continued)

6. Measure 480 g (1 lb 1 oz/2 cups) of sweet potato into a large mixing bowl. Add 250 ml (8½ fl oz/1 cup) of the cheese sauce to the mashed sweet potato and beat with a wooden spoon until smooth. Pour the remaining cheese sauce into the sweet potato and mix until smooth. Drain the macaroni and add to the mixture, stirring until it is coated in the sauce. If the mixture feels a little thick, add the remaining reserved sweet potato cooking water and stir well.

7. Divide the macaroni cheese between four 500 ml (17 fl oz/2 cup) ovenproof dishes and sprinkle the parmesan cheese and breadcrumbs on top. Place the dishes on a baking tray and bake until the filling is bubbling and the top is crispy, about 25 minutes. Alternatively, bake in a 2 litre (68 fl oz/8 cup) ovenproof dish for about 40 minutes.

new potatoes in parsley sauce

With the freshness of parsley – lots of it – this delicious, old-fashioned dish is one you might have had with corned beef at Grandma's house. You remember how good it was, so set the table with your best tablecloth and enjoy.

Use new potatoes.

1 kg (2 lb 3 oz) scrubbed new potatoes, the larger ones halved

1 teaspoon salt for the cooking water

500 ml (17 fl oz/2 cups) full-cream (whole) milk

60 g (2 oz) unsalted butter

50 g (1¾ oz/⅓ cup) plain (all-purpose) flour

30 g (1 oz/½ cup) finely chopped fresh flat-leaf (Italian) parsley

½ teaspoon sea salt

¼ teaspoon freshly ground black pepper

1. Put the potatoes and the salt in a large saucepan and cover with cold water. Bring to the boil over medium–high heat and boil until tender, about 12 minutes, testing with the point of a sharp knife. Drain the potatoes and return them to the saucepan over low heat for 1 minute to ensure any excess water has evaporated.

2. Meanwhile, heat the milk in a small saucepan over medium heat until almost boiling.

3. In a medium saucepan over medium heat, melt the butter and add the flour, stirring until smooth. Keep stirring over the heat for 2 minutes to cook out the floury taste. Remove from the heat and whisk in the hot milk, a little at a time. Continue to whisk as you add more milk and the sauce thickens.

4. When all the milk has been added, put the sauce back over medium heat until bubbling. Stir through the parsley, sea salt and pepper. Taste and add more sea salt and pepper if needed. Pour the sauce over the potatoes and stir gently until the potatoes are covered in the sauce.

5. Transfer the potatoes to a serving dish and serve immediately.

potato and ricotta gnocchi with brown butter and cherry tomatoes

This is just the gnocchi recipe you've been looking for. The addition of ricotta to the potato makes these gnocchi meltingly tender, and the cherry tomatoes soften into the browned butter for a brighter take on the traditional sauce. Timing is important, so have the sauce ready before you drop the gnocchi into the boiling water.

Use floury (starchy or roasting) potatoes; see pages 002–003 for a list of varieties.

for the gnocchi

3 medium potatoes, about 500 g (1 lb 2 oz)

½ teaspoon salt for the cooking water

1 large egg plus 1 yolk, whisked

185 g (6½ oz/¾ cup) ricotta

150 g (5½ oz/1 cup) plain (all-purpose) flour, sifted, plus extra for dusting

50 g (1¾ oz/½ cup) freshly grated parmesan cheese

¼ teaspoon sea salt

for the sauce

90 g (3 oz) unsalted butter

500 g (1 lb 2 oz) cherry tomatoes, halved

¼ teaspoon sea salt

¼ teaspoon freshly ground black pepper, plus extra to serve

1 tablespoon lemon juice

60 ml (2 fl oz /¼ cup) potato cooking water

10 g (¼ oz/⅓ cup) torn fresh basil leaves, loosely packed, plus a few extra, to serve

1. To start the gnocchi, peel and chop the potatoes into pieces, about 3 cm (1¼ in). Put in a small saucepan with the salt and cover with cold water. Bring to the boil over medium–high heat and cook until very tender, about 15 minutes, testing with the point of a sharp knife. Drain the potatoes, reserving 60 ml (2 fl oz/¼ cup) of the cooking water, and return them to the saucepan over low heat for 1 minute to ensure any excess water has evaporated. Pass the potato through a ricer or mash very well. Set aside to cool.

2. While the potatoes are cooking, bring a large saucepan of water to the boil over medium–high heat, ready to cook the gnocchi.

3. Start the sauce while the potatoes are cooling. Melt the butter in a small frying pan over medium heat. Cook the butter until it starts to brown, about 3 minutes. Stir in the tomatoes, salt and pepper and simmer on medium–low heat until the tomatoes become soft and start to melt into the butter, about 8 minutes. Stir in the lemon juice and 60 ml (2 fl oz /¼ cup) of the potato cooking water until combined. Taste and add more sea salt and pepper if needed. Reduce the heat to low and stir the sauce occasionally while you make the gnocchi.

4. While the sauce is simmering, measure 395 g (14 oz/1¾ cups) of the cooked, smooth potato into a large mixing bowl. Pass the ricotta through the ricer (or push it through a sieve) and add to the mixing bowl. Add the flour, 35 g (1½ oz/⅓ cup) of the parmesan cheese, the egg mixture and sea salt to the mixing bowl and mix with a spatula or your hand for as short a time as possible, just until the sticky dough starts to come together.

Recipe continues on next page.

potato and ricotta gnocchi with brown butter and cherry tomatoes (continued)

5. Tip the dough onto a lightly floured work surface and bring together in a rough ball. Divide the dough into 4 pieces and roll each quarter into a long cylinder that's about the width of your finger. Cut each roll of dough into 2 cm (¾ in) pieces and place them on a lightly floured tray while you roll and slice the remaining dough.

6. Cook half of the gnocchi in the large saucepan of boiling water over medium–high heat. When they rise to the surface, leave them for 20 seconds and then use a slotted spoon to transfer them to the tomato sauce. Add the basil and turn the gnocchi gently in the sauce. Repeat with the remaining gnocchi.

7. Transfer to a serving bowl. Garnish with the remaining parmesan cheese, basil and pepper and serve immediately.

beef, beer and potato stew

This is the sort of stew that would see you through an Irish winter. It's hearty, warm and delicious – classic winter comfort food. Try it with bread on the side to mop up the gravy.

Use new potatoes.

2 tablespoons plain (all-purpose) flour

700 g (1 lb 9 oz) braising/stewing beef, chopped into 3 cm (1¼ in) cubes

2 tablespoons vegetable oil

150 g (5½ oz) smoked speck (or use thick, smoked rindless bacon rashers/slices), chopped into thick matchsticks

1 large onion, diced

2 celery stalks, sliced

2 garlic cloves, finely diced

2 tablespoons tomato paste (concentrated purée)

2 teaspoons Vegemite, or use soy sauce

250 ml (8½ fl oz/1 cup) stout or other dark beer

1 litre (34 fl oz/4 cups) beef stock (low-salt)

750 g (1 lb 11 oz) new potatoes, quartered

1 medium parsnip, about 250 g (9 oz), woody core discarded, cut into small cubes

3 bay leaves

2 teaspoons chopped fresh rosemary

½ teaspoon freshly ground black pepper

to serve

1 tablespoon chopped fresh flat-leaf (Italian) parsley

1. Pour the flour in a sturdy plastic bag and add the beef pieces. Twist the top of the bag closed and shake it to coat the beef. Heat 1 tablespoon of the vegetable oil in a large heavy-based saucepan over medium–high heat and brown half of the beef, turning until all sides are coloured. Transfer the beef to a plate and repeat with the second tablespoon of oil and the remaining beef pieces.

2. Reduce the heat to medium and add the speck and onion. Fry until the onion is soft and the speck is starting to brown, about 5 minutes. Add the celery and garlic to the pan and fry for 2 minutes, until the garlic is fragrant. Stir through the tomato paste and Vegemite. Pour in the beer and stir for about 2 minutes, scraping the bottom of the pan to loosen any browned bits.

3. Pour in the beef stock and add the beef pieces, potatoes, parsnip, bay leaves, rosemary and pepper. Increase the heat to medium–high until bubbling. Reduce the heat to low and simmer, covered, for 2 hours, stirring occasionally.

4. Remove the lid and increase the heat to medium–low. Simmer for a further 30 minutes to 1 hour, stirring occasionally, until the sauce has thickened and the meat is very tender.

5. To serve, ladle the stew into shallow, wide bowls and sprinkle with parsley.

white fish and red potato stew

A favourite with my seafood-loving family, this stew is full of the classic flavours of tomatoes, potatoes and garlic. You won't taste the anchovies, which add a great depth of flavour that is essential. As it's cooked in one pot, you could even make it on a weeknight.

Use red-skinned new potatoes.

1 tablespoon olive oil

1 large onion, diced

1 medium fennel bulb, trimmed, cored and diced

2 celery stalks, sliced

1 large carrot, diced

3 garlic cloves, finely diced

1 tablespoon tomato paste (concentrated purée)

4 anchovies

250 ml (8½ fl oz/1 cup) white wine

1 litre (34 fl oz/4 cups) fish stock (low-salt), or use chicken or vegetable stock

600 g (1 lb 5 oz) potatoes, quartered

400 g (14 oz) tinned chopped tomatoes

10 g (14 oz/⅓ cup) chopped fresh flat-leaf (Italian) parsley, plus extra to serve

1 tablespoon lemon juice

1 teaspoon grated lemon zest

1 teaspoon paprika

1 teaspoon dried lemon thyme leaves, or use dried thyme leaves

½ teaspoon sea salt

¼ teaspoon freshly ground black pepper, plus extra to serve

750 g (1 lb 11 oz) firm white boneless fish (such as ling), chopped into 2.5 cm (1 in) pieces

to serve

crusty bread

1 lemon, cut into 6 wedges

1. Heat the olive oil in a large saucepan over medium heat and cook the onions, fennel, celery and carrot until softened, stirring occasionally, about 10 minutes. Add the garlic, tomato paste and anchovies and stir until the anchovies fall apart. Increase the heat to medium–high, add the white wine and bring to the boil. Stir in the stock, potatoes, tomatoes, parsley, lemon juice, lemon zest, paprika, lemon thyme, sea salt and pepper. Bring back to the boil, then reduce the heat to medium and simmer, stirring occasionally, until the potatoes are tender when tested with the point of a sharp knife, about 15 minutes.

2. Add the fish and simmer, stirring occasionally, until the fish pieces are opaque and cooked through, about 5 minutes. Taste and add more sea salt and pepper if needed.

3. Serve in shallow, wide bowls with plenty of bread on the side. Garnish each bowl with parsley, pepper and a wedge of lemon.

mash

mashed potato bake

When you can't decide if you'd like mashed potato or your favourite baked potato – the one with oodles of cheese, sour cream and bacon – this is the answer. Serve this with sausages and it's a real winner.

Use floury (starchy or roasting) potatoes; see pages 002–003 for a list of varieties.

90 g (3 oz) unsalted butter, chopped, plus extra to grease the casserole dish

12 medium potatoes, about 2 kg (4 lb 6 oz), peeled and cut into 3 cm (1¼ in) cubes

4 garlic cloves, peeled and left whole

1 teaspoon salt for the cooking water

200 g (7 oz) rindless bacon rashers (slices), chopped into 1.5 cm (½ in) pieces

6 spring onions (scallions), white and green parts sliced, root end discarded

375 g (13 oz/1½ cups) sour cream

375 g (13 oz/3 cups) grated cheddar cheese

½ teaspoon sea salt

½ teaspoon freshly ground black pepper

1. Preheat the oven to 190°C (375°F) and grease a large casserole dish, about 35 x 25 x 5 cm (13¾ x 10 x 2 in), or use 2 smaller casserole dishes if preferred.

2. Put the potatoes in a large saucepan with the garlic cloves and the salt and cover with cold water. Bring to the boil over medium–high heat and boil until very tender, about 15 minutes, testing with the point of a sharp knife. Drain the potatoes and garlic, reserving 250 ml (8½ fl oz/1 cup) of the cooking water, and return them to the saucepan over low heat for 2 minutes to ensure any excess water has evaporated.

3. Meanwhile, melt 30 g (1 oz) of the butter in a medium frying pan over medium heat and cook the bacon and spring onions until the bacon is starting to crisp and the spring onions are soft, about 8–10 minutes.

4. In a small saucepan over medium heat, melt the remaining 60 g (2 oz) of butter and whisk in the sour cream until steaming but not boiling. Add two-thirds of the cheese and stir until melted.

5. Mash the potatoes and garlic together until very smooth. Using a wooden spoon, stir in the sour cream mixture, the sea salt and pepper and beat until smooth. Stir in 60 ml (2 fl oz/ ¼ cup) of the cooking water, using more if needed, and beat until creamy.

6. Stir the bacon and spring onions into the potatoes. Taste and add more sea salt and pepper if needed. Transfer the potatoes to the prepared casserole dish with a light hand, keeping the top rough to maximise the crunchy bits. Sprinkle with the remaining cheese and bake until the top is golden, about 30 minutes.

buttermilk mashed potatoes

I like to make this mash when I'm baking oven-fried chicken – the tang of the buttermilk paired with potato makes for a decadently rich mash. Make sure you use lots of freshly ground black pepper.

Use floury (starchy or roasting) potatoes; see pages 002–003 for a list of varieties.

6 medium potatoes, about 1 kg (2 lb 3 oz), peeled and cut into 3 cm (1¼ in) pieces

½ teaspoon salt for the cooking water

60 g (2 oz) unsalted butter, melted

¼ teaspoon sea salt

¼ teaspoon freshly ground black pepper, to serve

250 ml (8½ fl oz/1 cup) buttermilk, at room temperature

to serve

1 tablespoon olive oil

1 tablespoon chopped fresh flat-leaf (Italian) parsley

1. Put the potatoes and salt in a medium saucepan and cover with cold water. Bring to the boil over medium–high heat and boil until very tender, about 15 minutes, testing with the point of a sharp knife. Drain the potatoes and return them to the saucepan over low heat for 1 minute to ensure any excess water has evaporated.

2. Mash the potatoes until smooth. Stir in the butter, sea salt and pepper. Add the buttermilk and beat until creamy. Taste and add more sea salt and pepper if needed.

3. Transfer to a serving dish, drizzle with olive oil and sprinkle with parsley and pepper. Serve immediately.

classic mashed potatoes

Classic mashed potatoes are not only the ultimate comfort food, but also the perfect side dish for a happy family dinner. Lamb chops, pork chops, steak, fish – everything is better with mash. I love it with a simple fried egg on top and freshly ground black pepper. Or a drizzle of gravy. You get the picture.

Use floury (starchy or roasting) potatoes; see pages 002–003 for a list of varieties.

6 medium potatoes, about 1 kg (2 lb 3 oz), peeled and cut into 3 cm (1¼ in) pieces

½ teaspoon salt for the cooking water

80 g (2¾ oz) unsalted butter

250 ml (8½ fl oz/1 cup) full-cream (whole) milk

¼ teaspoon sea salt

¼ teaspoon freshly ground black pepper, plus extra to serve

1. Put the potatoes and the salt in a medium saucepan and cover with cold water. Bring to the boil over medium–high heat and boil until very tender, about 15 minutes, testing with the point of a sharp knife. Drain the potatoes and return them to the saucepan over low heat for 1 minute to ensure any excess water has evaporated.

2. Meanwhile, in a small saucepan over medium heat, melt the butter. Whisk in the milk and stir until steaming but not boiling, about 2 minutes.

3. Pass the potatoes through a ricer or mash until very smooth. With a wooden spoon, stir in the milk and butter mixture, sea salt and pepper and beat until creamy. Taste and add more sea salt and pepper if needed.

4. Transfer to a serving dish and sprinkle with extra freshly ground black pepper. Serve immediately.

potato, apple and bacon mash

Take everything that works so well with pork chops – potatoes, apples, garlic – and combine them in one perfect dish. Serve as a side, or as the ultimate comfort food.

Use floury (starchy or roasting) potatoes; see pages 002–003 for a list of varieties.

6 medium potatoes, about 1 kg (2 lb 3 oz), peeled and cut into 3 cm (1¼ in) pieces

2 medium granny smith apples or other tart cooking apples, peeled, cored and cut into pieces

½ teaspoon salt for the cooking water

40 g (1½ oz) unsalted butter

100 g (3½ oz) rindless bacon rashers (slices), chopped into 1 cm (½ in) pieces

250 ml (8½ fl oz/1 cup) full-cream (whole) milk, warmed

60 g (2 oz/½ cup) grated cheddar cheese

½ teaspoon sea salt

¼ teaspoon freshly ground black pepper

to serve

1 tablespoon finely sliced fresh chives

1. Put the potatoes, apples and salt in a medium saucepan and cover with cold water. Bring to the boil over medium–high heat and boil until very tender, about 15 minutes, testing with the point of a sharp knife. Drain the potatoes and apples, reserving 250 ml (8½ fl oz/1 cup) of the cooking water, and return them to the saucepan over low heat for 1 minute to ensure any excess water has evaporated.

2. Meanwhile, melt 10 g (¼ oz) of the butter in a small frying pan over medium heat and cook the bacon until crispy, about 5 minutes, stirring occasionally.

3. Melt the remaining butter in a small saucepan over medium heat and whisk in the milk. When steaming, add the cheese, sea salt and pepper and stir until the cheese is melted.

4. Mash the potatoes and apples together until smooth. Add the milk mixture and beat with a wooden spoon until creamy. Scrape the bacon, any crispy bits and remaining fat in the frying pan into the potatoes and stir until combined. Taste and add more sea salt and pepper if needed.

5. Transfer to a serving dish and sprinkle with the chives. Serve immediately.

spring onion mashed potatoes

The spring onions (scallions) add a freshness that makes this the perfect side dish for fish. Leftover spring onion mash is also excellent with a fried egg on top for a fine, easy dinner.

Use floury (starchy or roasting) potatoes; see pages 002–003 for a list of varieties.

6 medium potatoes, about 1 kg (2 lb 3 oz), peeled and cut into 3 cm (1¼ in) pieces

½ teaspoon salt for the cooking water

60 g (2 oz) unsalted butter, melted

½ teaspoon sea salt

¼ teaspoon freshly ground black pepper

250 ml (8½ fl oz/1 cup) full-cream (whole) milk

8 spring onions (scallions), white and green parts finely sliced, root end discarded

25 g (1 oz/¼ cup) grated parmesan cheese

1. Put the potatoes and salt in a medium saucepan and cover with cold water. Bring to the boil over medium–high heat and boil until very tender, about 15 minutes, testing with the point of a sharp knife. Drain the potatoes and return them to the saucepan over low heat for 1 minute to ensure any excess water has evaporated. Mash well. Using a wooden spoon, stir in the butter, sea salt and pepper and beat until very smooth.

2. Meanwhile, heat the milk and spring onions in a small saucepan over medium heat until the milk is steaming and starting to bubble. Remove from the heat and allow to infuse for 5 minutes. Add spring onions mixture and parmesan cheese to the mashed potatoes. With a wooden spoon, beat until creamy. Taste and add more sea salt and pepper if needed.

3. Transfer to a serving dish and serve immediately.

potato, parmesan and mustard mash

The mustardy tang of this mash goes particularly well with steak and is always a winner at my place. Give it a try the next time you have a barbecue.

Use floury (starchy or roasting) potatoes; see pages 002–003 for a list of varieties.

6 medium potatoes, about 1 kg (2 lb 3 oz), peeled and cut into 3 cm (1¼ in) pieces

½ teaspoon salt for the cooking water

2 garlic cloves, peeled and left whole

60 g (2 oz) unsalted butter, cubed

125 g (4½ oz/½ cup) sour cream

50 g (1¾ oz/½ cup) grated parmesan cheese

1 tablespoon wholegrain mustard

½ teaspoon sea salt

¼ teaspoon freshly ground black pepper

1. Put the potatoes, salt and garlic in a medium saucepan and cover with cold water. Bring to the boil over medium–high heat and boil until very tender, about 15 minutes, testing with the point of a sharp knife. Drain the potatoes and garlic, reserving 250 ml (8½ fl oz/ 1 cup) of the cooking water, and return them to the saucepan over low heat for 1 minute to ensure any excess water has evaporated. Mash until smooth.

2. Meanwhile, in a small saucepan over medium–low heat, melt the butter and stir in the sour cream until combined. Add the parmesan, mustard, sea salt and pepper and stir until the cheese is melted.

3. Add the sour cream mixture to the garlicky mashed potatoes and stir until smooth. Add 60 ml (2 fl oz/¼ cup) of the cooking water and stir until creamy, adding more water if needed. Taste and add more sea salt and pepper if needed.

4. Transfer to a serving dish and take to the table. This mash needs no adornment.

sweet potato mash with brown butter and thyme

Maybe not one for the mash purists, but this sweet potato mash, with its nutty brown butter and bright notes of thyme, is the perfect accompaniment to roast beef.

Use orange sweet potatoes.

2 large sweet potatoes, about 1.3 kg (2 lb 14 oz), peeled and cut into 3 cm (1¼ in) pieces

½ teaspoon salt for the cooking water

60 g (2 oz) unsalted butter

25 g (1 oz/¼ cup) grated parmesan cheese

2 tablespoons sour cream

2 teaspoons fresh thyme leaves, plus extra to serve

1 teaspoon balsamic vinegar

½ teaspoon sea salt

¼ teaspoon freshly ground pepper, plus extra to serve

1. Put the sweet potatoes and salt in a large saucepan and cover with cold water. Bring to the boil over medium–high heat and boil until very tender, about 15 minutes, testing with the point of a sharp knife. Drain, reserving 250 ml (8½ fl oz/1 cup) of the cooking water, and return them to the saucepan over low heat for 1 minute to ensure any excess water has evaporated. Mash until smooth.

2. Meanwhile, melt the butter in a small frying pan over medium–low heat. Stir occasionally as it darkens. When it's ready the butter will be the colour of weak tea and will smell nutty. This may take up to 10 minutes, so be patient, but don't leave it unattended.

3. Pour the browned butter into the sweet potato mash, making sure to scrape up the dark bits at the bottom of the frying pan, and stir through with the parmesan, sour cream, thyme, balsamic vinegar, sea salt and pepper. Taste and add more sea salt and pepper if needed. Add 60 ml (2 fl oz/¼ cup) of the cooking water and beat well with a wooden spoon until creamy, adding more cooking water if needed.

4. Transfer to a serving dish, sprinkle with thyme and pepper and serve immediately.

potato and olive mash

This garlic and olive rendition takes mashed potato to new heights of flavour. It's great with steak or roast chicken.

Use floury (starchy or roasting) potatoes; see pages 002–003 for a list of varieties.

6 medium potatoes, about 1 kg (2 lb 3 oz), peeled and cut into 3 cm (1¼ in) pieces

3 garlic cloves, peeled and left whole

½ teaspoon salt for the cooking water

60 ml (2 fl oz/¼ cup) olive oil, plus extra to serve

35 g (1¼ oz/⅓ cup) grated parmesan cheese

¼ teaspoon sea salt

¼ teaspoon freshly ground black pepper, plus extra to serve

80 g (2¾ oz) kalamata olives, pitted and chopped

to serve

1 teaspoon fresh thyme leaves

1. Put the potatoes, garlic and salt in a medium saucepan and cover with cold water. Bring to the boil over medium–high heat and boil until very tender, about 15 minutes, testing with the point of a sharp knife. Drain the potatoes and garlic, reserving 250 ml (8½ fl oz/1 cup) of the cooking water, and return them to the saucepan over low heat for 1 minute to ensure any excess water has evaporated. Mash until smooth.

2. With a wooden spoon, stir the olive oil, parmesan, sea salt and pepper into the potatoes until smooth. Beat in enough of the reserved cooking water to give a creamy consistency, starting with 125 ml (4 fl oz/½ cup). Stir in the olives. Taste and add more sea salt and pepper if required.

3. Transfer to a serving dish and drizzle with extra olive oil, if desired. Sprinkle with thyme and pepper and serve immediately.

anchovy and cheese mash

The subtle background notes of anchovies and the nutty jarlsberg cheese add a surprising depth of flavour to this mash. It holds its own with a steak and a robust sauce, and is equally happy paired with salmon.

Use floury (starchy or roasting) potatoes; see pages 002–003 for a list of varieties.

6 medium potatoes, about 1 kg (2 lb 3 oz), peeled and cut into 3 cm (1¼ in) pieces

1 garlic clove, peeled and left whole

½ teaspoon salt for the cooking water

60 g (2 oz) unsalted butter

3 anchovies

250 ml (8½ fl oz/1 cup) full-cream (whole) milk

195 g (7 oz/1½ cups) grated jarlsberg or gruyère cheese

1 teaspoon chopped fresh rosemary leaves, plus extra to serve

½ teaspoon freshly ground black pepper

sea salt

1. Put the potatoes, garlic and salt in a small saucepan and cover with cold water. Bring to the boil over medium–high heat and boil until very tender, about 15 minutes, testing with the point of a sharp knife. Drain the potatoes and garlic, reserving 250 ml (8½ fl oz/1 cup) of the cooking water, and return them to the saucepan over low heat for 1 minute to ensure any excess water has evaporated. Mash until smooth.

2. Meanwhile, melt the butter in a small saucepan over medium heat and add the anchovies, squashing them into the butter until almost dissolved. Whisk in the milk and stir until warmed but not boiling.

3. With a wooden spoon, stir the milk mixture, jarlsberg, rosemary and pepper into the potatoes until smooth. Beat in enough of the reserved cooking water to give a creamy consistency, starting with 125 ml (4 fl oz/½ cup). Taste and add sea salt and more pepper if required.

4. Transfer to a serving dish, scatter with extra rosemary leaves and serve immediately.

cauliflower cheese potato mash

I'm not alone when I say that my favourite way to eat cauliflower is slathered in cheese sauce. Add them to mashed potato and it's a winning combination.

Use floury (starchy or roasting) potatoes; see pages 002–003 for a list of varieties.

6 medium potatoes, about 1 kg (2 lb 3 oz), peeled and cut into 3 cm (1¼ in) pieces

½ small cauliflower, about 400 g (14 oz), trimmed and chopped into 1.5 cm (½ in) pieces

½ teaspoon salt for the cooking water

2 bay leaves

45 g (1½ oz) unsalted butter, chopped

160 g (5½ oz/⅔ cup) sour cream

75 g (2¾ oz/¾ cup) grated parmesan cheese

½ teaspoon sea salt

¼ teaspoon freshly ground black pepper

to serve

1 tablespoon finely chopped fresh flat-leaf (Italian) parsley

1. Put the potatoes, cauliflower and salt in a large saucepan with the bay leaves and cover with cold water. Bring to the boil over medium–high heat and boil until very tender, about 15 minutes, testing with the point of a sharp knife. Drain the potatoes and cauliflower, reserving about 250 ml (8½ fl oz/ 1 cup) of the cooking water, and return to the saucepan over a low heat for 1 minute to ensure any excess water has evaporated. Discard the bay leaves. Pass the potatoes and cauliflower through a ricer, or mash until very smooth.

2. Meanwhile, in a small saucepan over medium–low heat, melt the butter and stir in the sour cream until combined. Add the parmesan, sea salt and pepper and stir until the cheese is melted.

3. Add the sour cream mixture to the mashed potatoes and cauliflower and stir until smooth. Add 60 ml (2 fl oz/¼ cup) of the cooking water and stir until creamy, adding more water if needed. Taste for seasoning and add more sea salt and pepper if needed.

4. Transfer to a serving dish and sprinkle with parsley to serve.

bake & roast

super easy, super crispy potato peels

The next time you're peeling potatoes, don't throw away the peels. Baked in the oven, they make a crunchy, moreish snack or a great topping for soup. The secret is to wash and dry them well, toss them in oil and get them into the oven quickly. They're so good, and so easy, you'll wonder why you haven't been doing it for years.

Use well-washed potato peels.

about 100 g (3½ oz) potato peels, from about 1 kg (2 lb 3 oz) peeled potatoes

1 tablespoon olive oil

½ teaspoon sea salt flakes, plus extra to serve

1. Preheat the oven to 210°C (410°F). Line a baking tray with baking paper.

2. Wash the potatoes well before you peel them. As you peel each potato, give the peels a rinse and put them in a colander to drain. Dry them well on paper towel and put them in a small mixing bowl. Add the olive oil and salt and turn the peels over until they are well coated.

3. Place them on the baking tray and bake until golden and crispy, about 20–25 minutes.

4. Tip the crispy potato peels onto a plate and serve immediately with a sprinkle of extra sea salt if desired.

dinosaur potatoes

Okay, there are no dinosaurs in this potato bake. The vertical potato slices might look like a reptilian spine but the taste is classic dauphinoise – crispy on the top and creamy underneath. Serve with roast chicken or lamb and a big green salad, or even with just the salad. Delicious.

Use waxy potatoes; see pages 002–003 for a list of varieties.

30 g (1 oz) unsalted butter, plus extra to grease the casserole dish

2 anchovies

330 ml (11 fl oz/1⅓ cups) thick (heavy) cream

50 g (1¾ oz/½ cup) freshly grated parmesan cheese

2 garlic cloves, peeled and left whole

1 bay leaf

1 teaspoon fresh thyme leaves, plus extra to serve

½ teaspoon sea salt

½ teaspoon freshly ground black pepper

⅛ teaspoon freshly grated nutmeg

6 medium potatoes, about 1 kg (2 lb 3 oz)

1. Preheat the oven to 190°C (375°F) and grease a small casserole dish, about 20 x 15 x 6 cm (8 x 6 x 2½ in).

2. Melt the butter in a large saucepan over medium heat and add the anchovies, stirring and squashing them until they almost melt into the butter. Add the cream, half the parmesan, the garlic, bay leaf, thyme, salt, pepper and nutmeg and bring to the boil, stirring. Remove from the heat and allow the flavours to infuse for 5 minutes, then discard the garlic cloves and bay leaf.

3. Peel the potatoes and cut them into 3 mm (⅛ in) slices. Immediately drop them into the cream mixture and stir gently to ensure each slice is covered in cream. Using tongs, pick up stacks of potato slices and place them vertically in staggered rows in the casserole dish. Pour some or all of the sauce that remains in the saucepan into the casserole dish, ensuring that the tops of the potato slices protrude from the sauce by about 1.5 cm (½ in) so they will brown. Cover the dish with foil, place on a baking tray in the oven and bake for 1 hour.

4. Remove the foil and scatter the top of the potatoes with the remaining parmesan. Bake until the potatoes are tender, with crisp tops where their dinosaur spines poke out of the cream. This should take about a further 30 minutes.

5. Serve immediately, sprinkled with additional thyme leaves.

red potato chips

Home-made potato chips. Yes, please. They taste so crispy and salty you may never want to go back to packet chips again. If you can find them, use red-fleshed fingerling potatoes for spectacular ruby chips. Try them as a soup topper on a puréed soup.

Use red-skinned new or fingerling potatoes.

500 g (1 lb 2 oz) potatoes

2 tablespoons olive oil

1 teaspoon sea salt flakes, plus extra to serve

1. Pour 500 ml (17 fl oz/2 cups) of cold water into a large mixing bowl.

2. Scrub the potatoes and cut them into thin slices, about 2 mm (1/10 in). Drop the slices into the water, turning them to ensure they aren't stuck together. Leave the slices in the water for 30 minutes, then rinse and drain in a colander. Dry the slices well on paper towel.

3. Meanwhile, preheat the oven to 150°C (300°F) and line 3 baking trays with baking paper.

4. Combine the olive oil and sea salt flakes in a large mixing bowl. Tip in the potato slices and toss, using 2 forks, until they are coated in oil. Place the slices on the baking trays, ensuring they are not overlapping.

5. Bake for 25 minutes, then turn the chips over. Swap the trays around when you return them to the oven. Start checking the chips every few minutes after a total of about 50 minutes in the oven. The edges will darken and they should feel crisp or almost crisp when they are done, about 50–60 minutes (they will crisp up further as they cool on the trays).

6. When cool, put the chips into a serving dish, sprinkle with extra sea salt flakes and serve.

sweet potato chips

These sweet potato chips are deliciously moreish and so easy to make. Eat them as they are or serve with your favourite dip. Guacamole anyone?

Use orange sweet potatoes.

4–5 long thin sweet potatoes, about 500 g
  (1 lb 2 oz)

2 tablespoons olive oil

½ teaspoon sea salt flakes, plus extra to serve

½ teaspoon cumin, or use smoky paprika

¼ teaspoon freshly ground black pepper

1. Pour 500 ml (17 fl oz/2 cups) of cold water into a large mixing bowl.

2. Peel the sweet potatoes and cut them into thin slices, about 2 mm (⅒ in). Drop the slices into the water, turning them to ensure they aren't stuck together. Leave the slices in the water for 60 minutes, then rinse and drain in a colander. Dry the slices well on paper towel.

3. Meanwhile, preheat the oven to 150°C (300°F) and line 3 baking trays with baking paper.

4. Combine the olive oil, sea salt flakes, cumin and pepper in a large mixing bowl. Tip in the sweet potato slices and toss, using 2 forks, until they are coated in oil. Place the slices on the baking trays, ensuring they are not overlapping.

5. Bake for 20 minutes, then turn the chips over. Swap the trays around when you return them to the oven. Start checking the chips every few minutes after a total of about 40 minutes in the oven. The edges will darken and they should feel crisp or almost crisp when they are done, about 40–50 minutes (they will crisp up further as they cool on the trays).

6. When cool, put the chips into a serving dish, sprinkle with extra sea salt flakes and serve.

spicy oven-baked potato wedges

Whenever I make these, they barely hit the serving plate before they disappear. They are so easy, older kids can cook them after school. The hardest part is waiting for them to be ready.

Use floury (starchy or roasting) potatoes; see pages 002–003 for a list of varieties.

60 ml (2 fl oz/¼ cup) olive oil

1 teaspoon sea salt flakes, plus extra to serve

1 teaspoon grated lemon zest

½ teaspoon freshly ground black pepper

½ teaspoon dried oregano

½ teaspoon cayenne pepper, or to taste

5 medium potatoes, about 900 g (2 lb)

1. Preheat the oven to 220°C (430°F). Put 2 baking trays in the oven to heat.

2. In a large mixing bowl, combine the olive oil with the sea salt flakes, lemon zest, pepper, oregano and cayenne pepper.

3. Wash the potatoes well and cut them into halves lengthways, then cut each half into 4 long wedges. Dry them on paper towel, then add to the mixing bowl and toss until all the wedges are coated with the spicy oil.

4. Line the hot baking trays with baking paper and divide the wedges between the 2 trays, cut side down. Pour any oil that remains in the mixing bowl over the wedges.

5. Bake, turning once, until the wedges are golden, about 25–30 minutes.

6. Tip them onto a plate and serve immediately, sprinkled with sea salt flakes.

toasty roast potatoes

You could have these as a side, or treat yourself and make them as a snack, perfect on a wintery afternoon. After school or after work, these will warm you up from the inside out.

Use floury (starchy or roasting) potatoes; see pages 002–003 for a list of varieties.

6 medium potatoes, about 1 kg (2 lb 3 oz)

1 teaspoon salt for the cooking water

60 g (2 oz) melted butter

1 teaspoon curry powder

½ teaspoon sea salt

½ teaspoon cayenne pepper, or to taste

¼ teaspoon freshly ground black pepper

to serve

sea salt flakes

1. Preheat the oven to 210°C (410°F). Adjust the oven racks so there is one at the top of the oven and one at the bottom. Put 2 baking trays in the oven to heat.

2. Peel the potatoes and cut each in half lengthways. Cut each half into 2–3 pieces, depending on the size of the potato, making all the pieces a similar size.

3. Put the potato pieces and the salt in a medium saucepan and cover with cold water. Bring to the boil over medium–high heat and boil until just tender, about 15 minutes, testing with the point of a sharp knife. Drain the potatoes and return to the saucepan over low heat for 1 minute to ensure any excess water has evaporated. To rough up the edges, carefully stir the potatoes with a large metal spoon so they bash against each other.

4. Melt the butter in a small saucepan over medium heat. Pour the melted butter over the potatoes, turning carefully with a large metal spoon until all the potatoes are coated in butter.

5. In a small mixing bowl, stir together the curry powder, sea salt, cayenne pepper and pepper. Sprinkle this mixture over the buttered potatoes and turn them until they are coated in the spice mix.

6. Remove the hot trays from the oven and line them with baking paper. Place the potatoes onto the trays and into the oven.

7. Bake until the potatoes are golden and crisp, about 45–50 minutes, turning them and swapping the trays after about 30 minutes.

8. Place the potatoes in a serving dish, sprinkle with sea salt flakes and serve immediately.

crispy duck fat roast potatoes

These are so good that you'll probably need to allow extra per person. Crunchy on the outside and soft inside, the secret to these potatoes is boiling them first, roughing up the edges and tossing them in hot duck fat before baking. No garlic, no herbs, just beautiful potatoes.

Use floury (starchy or roasting) potatoes; see pages 002–003 for a list of varieties.

6 medium potatoes, about 1 kg (2 lb 3 oz)

1 teaspoon salt for the cooking water

60 g (2 oz) rendered duck fat, or use melted butter

to serve

1 teaspoon sea salt flakes

1. Preheat the oven to 220°C (430°F). Adjust the oven racks so there is one at the top of the oven and one at the bottom. Put 2 baking trays in the oven to heat.

2. Peel the potatoes and cut each in half lengthways. Cut each half into 2–3 pieces, depending on the size of the potato, making all the pieces a similar size.

3. Put the potato pieces and the salt in a medium saucepan and cover with cold water. Bring to the boil over medium–high heat and boil until just tender, about 15 minutes, testing with the point of a sharp knife. Drain the potatoes and return to the saucepan over low heat for 1 minute to ensure any excess water has evaporated. To rough up the edges, carefully stir the potatoes with a large metal spoon so they bash against each other. Don't worry if a few small bits fall off, as they will be extra crispy.

4. Heat the duck fat in a small saucepan over medium heat until you can see small bubbles rising to the surface, about 1–2 minutes.

5. Pour the duck fat over the potatoes and, with a large metal spoon, turn the potatoes until they are coated. The potatoes may look a bit mushy around the edges but they will crisp up beautifully.

6. Remove the hot trays from the oven and line them with baking paper. Place the potatoes onto the trays and into the oven.

7. Bake until the potatoes are golden and crisp, about 45–50 minutes, turning them after about 30 minutes.

8. Place the potatoes in a serving dish, sprinkle with sea salt flakes and serve immediately.

sweet potato oven fries with lime coriander dipping sauce

Oven-baked sweet potato fries sing with a zingy lime dipping sauce. It's the perfect game-day snack. You just might need to double the recipe.

Use orange sweet potato.

for the fries

1 large sweet potato, about 650 g (1 lb 7 oz), peeled and cut into chips, about 1 cm (½ in) thick

2 tablespoons polenta

1 teaspoon sea salt

½ teaspoon smoked paprika, or use ground cumin

¼ teaspoon freshly ground black pepper

2 tablespoons olive oil

for the dipping sauce

125 ml (4 fl oz/½ cup) mayonnaise

½ small garlic clove, finely chopped

2 tablespoons finely chopped fresh coriander (cilantro) leaves

3 teaspoons lime juice

½ teaspoon grated lime zest

½ teaspoon Tabasco or other hot sauce, or to taste

½ teaspoon sea salt

¼ teaspoon freshly ground black pepper

1. Put the sweet potato chips in a large mixing bowl, cover with cold water and leave for 30 minutes. Rinse and drain the sweet potatoes in a colander, then tip them onto paper towel to dry. Blot any remaining visible moisture with paper towel.

2. Preheat the oven to 210°C (410°F). Adjust the oven racks so there is one at the top of the oven and one at the bottom. Put 2 baking trays in the oven to heat.

3. In a small mixing bowl, whisk or stir the polenta, sea salt, paprika and pepper until combined.

4. In a large mixing bowl, toss the sweet potato chips in the oil until each chip is coated. Tip the polenta/spice mix over the chips and toss well, until all the chips are well coated.

5. Remove the baking trays from the oven and line with baking paper. Spread half of the chips on each tray, making sure there is plenty of room between the chips. Bake for 20 minutes, then turn the chips and rotate the trays. Bake until the edges of the chips are turning dark, about 15–20 minutes more.

6. Meanwhile, make the dipping sauce. In a small mixing bowl, stir together the mayonnaise, garlic, coriander, lime juice, lime zest, Tabasco, salt and pepper.

7. To serve, place the fries on a plate with the dipping sauce in a small dish on the side.

coddled eggs with cauliflower cheese potato mash

What's the best way to lift an already amazing cauliflower cheese mashed potato? Add an egg. It's brilliant for brunch with toast soldiers on the side for dipping.

Use floury (starchy or roasting) potatoes; see pages 002–003 for a list of varieties.

25 g (1 oz) unsalted butter, plus extra to grease the ramekins

3 medium potatoes, about 500 g (1 lb 2 oz), peeled and cut into 2 cm (¾ in) pieces

¼ cauliflower head, about 200 g (7 oz), trimmed and cut into 1–1.5 cm (½ in) pieces

½ teaspoon salt for the cooking water

1 bay leaf

90 g (3 oz/⅓ cup) sour cream

50 g (1¾ oz/½ cup) finely grated parmesan cheese

¼ teaspoon sea salt

¹⁄₁₀ teaspoon freshly ground black pepper, plus extra for serving

6 large eggs

120 ml (4 fl oz) thick (heavy) cream

to serve

3 teaspoons finely chopped fresh flat-leaf (Italian) parsley

toasted bread slices, cut into strips

1. Preheat the oven to 180°C (350°F) and grease six 375 ml (12½ fl oz/1½ cup) capacity ramekins or ovenproof mason jars.

2. Put the potatoes and cauliflower in a saucepan with the salt and bay leaf and cover with cold water. Bring to the boil over medium–high heat and boil until very tender, about 15 minutes, testing with the point of a sharp knife. Drain the potatoes and cauliflower, reserving about 60 ml (2 fl oz/¼ cup) of the cooking water, and return them to the saucepan over low heat for 1 minute to ensure any excess water has evaporated. Discard the bay leaf and put the potatoes and cauliflower through a ricer, or mash until very smooth.

3. Meanwhile, in a small saucepan over medium–low heat, melt 20 g (¾ oz) of butter and stir in the sour cream until combined. Add 35 g (1¼ oz/⅓ cup) of the parmesan, the salt and pepper and stir until the cheese is melted.

4. Add the sour cream mixture to the mashed potatoes and cauliflower and stir until smooth. Add 1 tablespoon of the cooking water and stir until creamy, adding more water if needed. Taste for seasoning and add more salt and pepper if needed.

5. Divide the mash among the ramekins. Carefully crack 1 egg into each ramekin on top of the mash. Spoon 1 tablespoon of cream over each egg.

6. Place the ramekins in a large baking pan about 8 cm (3¼ in) deep. Carefully pour hot water into the baking pan to a depth of about 3–4 cm (1¼–1½ in). Bake until the egg whites are just set and the yolks still runny, about 15–17 minutes.

7. Carefully remove the ramekins from the baking pan and sprinkle each egg with the remaining parmesan, parsley and pepper. Serve with toast soldiers on the side.

classic potato bake

This classic potato bake is one of my go-to recipes when feeding a crowd. Not only does it look impressive and taste fantastic – creamy potatoes, bacon, cheese, crispy on top – it can be prepared in advance so all you have to do is put it in the oven while you grill some steaks and make a salad. Voila!

Use waxy potatoes; see pages 002–003 for a list of varieties.

12 medium potatoes, about 2 kg (4 lb 6 oz)

1 teaspoon salt for the cooking water

30 g (1 oz) unsalted butter, plus extra to grease the casserole dish

300 g (10½ oz) rindless bacon rashers (slices), chopped into 1 cm (½ in) slices

12 spring onions (scallions), white and green parts sliced, root ends discarded

500 g (1 lb 2 oz/2 cups) sour cream

375 g (13 oz/3 cups) grated cheddar cheese

½ teaspoon freshly ground black pepper

sea salt

1. Preheat the oven to 190°C (375°F) and grease a large casserole dish, about 35 x 25 x 5 cm (13¾ x 10 x 2 in).

2. Wash the potatoes and cut them in half lengthways. Slice each half into 1 cm (½ in) slices. Put the potato slices in a large saucepan with the salt and cover with cold water. Bring to the boil over high heat and boil until just tender, about 8–10 minutes, testing with the point of a sharp knife. Drain the potatoes, reserving about 250 ml (8½ fl oz/1 cup) of the cooking water, and return them to the saucepan over low heat for 2 minutes to ensure any excess water has evaporated. Transfer the potato slices to the casserole dish.

3. Meanwhile, melt the butter in a frying pan over medium heat and cook the bacon and spring onions, stirring occasionally, until the bacon is starting to turn golden and the spring onions are soft, about 10 minutes. Add the sour cream and stir until it starts to bubble, reducing the heat to medium–low if the sauce is catching on the bottom of the frying pan. Add 250 g (9 oz/2 cups) of the cheese and the pepper and stir until the cheese has melted into the sauce. Stir in 125 ml (4 fl/½ cup) of the potato cooking water until the sauce is smooth and the consistency of thick cream, adding more water as needed. Taste and add sea salt and more pepper if needed.

4. Pour the sauce over the potatoes. Using a large metal spoon, gently turn the potatoes until they are covered in sauce. Sprinkle the remaining cheese over the top of the potatoes and bake until bubbling and the cheese on top is melted and golden, about 30–40 minutes.

5. Allow to stand for 5 minutes before serving.

potato and caramelised onion gratin

A beautiful gratin needs little introduction. With its caramelised onions and combination of chicken stock and cream, this one is full of flavour and a lighter take on a classic dish. It's the perfect side for roast chicken or turkey.

Use waxy potatoes; see pages 002–003 for a list of varieties.

2 tablespoons olive oil

30 g (1 oz) unsalted butter

2 large onions, halved and thinly sliced

1 teaspoon finely chopped fresh rosemary

1 teaspoon fresh thyme leaves, plus extra to serve

190 ml (6½ fl oz/¾ cup) thick (heavy) cream

190 ml (6½ fl oz/¾ cup) chicken stock (low-salt)

½ teaspoon sea salt

½ teaspoon freshly ground black pepper

6 medium potatoes, about 1 kg (2 lb 3 oz)

1. Preheat the oven to 180°C (350°F) and grease a large baking pan, about 30 x 20 x 5 cm (12 x 8 x 2 in).

2. Heat the olive oil and butter in a medium frying pan over medium heat. Add the sliced onions and fry, stirring occasionally, until there are touches of gold on the onions, about 4 minutes. Reduce the heat to medium–low and cook, stirring occasionally, until the onions are very soft and golden brown, about 20 minutes. Remove from the heat and stir in the rosemary and thyme.

3. In a medium mixing bowl, whisk the cream, stock, sea salt and pepper together until smooth.

4. Scrub the potatoes and slice them thinly. Layer one-third of the potatoes in the baking pan. Top with half the onions and gently pour over one-third of the cream mixture. Repeat with another one-third of the potatoes and the remaining onions and pour over a further third of the cream mixture. Finish with the remaining potatoes and the remaining cream mixture. Gently press down on the potatoes with a spatula.

5. Cover with foil and bake for 1 hour. Remove the foil and bake until the potatoes are tender and the top is golden, about 30 minutes.

6. Allow to stand for 5 minutes. To serve, sprinkle with thyme.

crunchy potato and egg bake

This brings back memories of the mashed potatoes and eggs my mum used to make for an easy Sunday night dinner. The sour cream gives a nicely tart edge and the breadcrumbs make the whole thing a bit more glamorous. Although usually a side dish – it's good with lamb or chicken – I can easily eat a serving of this by itself!

Use waxy potatoes; see pages 002–003 for a list of varieties.

9 medium potatoes, about 1.5 kg (3 lb 5 oz)

1 teaspoon salt for the cooking water

90 g (3 oz) unsalted butter

375 g (13 oz/1½ cups) sour cream

185 g (6½ oz/1½ cups) grated cheddar cheese

½ teaspoon sea salt

½ teaspoon freshly ground black pepper

8 large eggs, hard-boiled

40 g (1½ oz/⅔ cup) panko (Japanese-style) breadcrumbs

1. Preheat the oven to 190°C (375°F) and grease a large casserole dish, about 35 x 25 x 5 cm (13¾ x 10 x 2 in).

2. Wash the potatoes well (peel if you prefer) and cut into 7 mm (¼ in) slices.

3. Put the potato slices and salt in a large saucepan and cover with cold water. Bring to the boil over medium–high heat and boil until just tender, about 8 minutes, testing with the point of a sharp knife. Drain the potatoes and return to the saucepan over low heat for 2 minutes to ensure any excess water has evaporated.

4. Melt the butter in a medium saucepan over medium heat. Add the sour cream and whisk until smooth and just bubbling. Remove from the heat and stir in half the grated cheese, the sea salt and pepper, until the cheese has melted into the sauce.

5. Cut the hard-boiled eggs into 5 mm (¼ in) slices.

6. Layer half of the potato slices in the casserole dish and cover with the egg slices. Pour over half of the sour cream mixture and layer with the remaining potato slices. Pour over the remaining sour cream mixture. Sprinkle the top evenly with the panko breadcrumbs and the remaining grated cheese.

7. Bake until the top is golden and crunchy and the filling is bubbling, about 30–40 minutes.

8. Stand for 5 minutes before serving.

potato, anchovy and rosemary soufflés

Soufflés look spectacular and will impress everyone at the table. A green salad on the side is almost essential. I often make a rocket and pear salad as a lovely side for these soufflés.

Use floury (starchy or roasting) potatoes; see pages 002–003 for a list of varieties.

50 g (1¾ oz) unsalted butter, plus extra to grease the ramekins

20 g (¾ oz/⅓ cup) panko (Japanese-style) breadcrumbs

3 medium potatoes, about 500 g (1 lb 2 oz), peeled and cut into 2 cm (¾ in) pieces

2 garlic cloves, peeled and left whole

½ teaspoon salt for the cooking water

4 anchovies

190 ml (6½ fl oz/¾ cup) buttermilk, at room temperature

100 g (3½ oz/1 cup) finely grated parmesan cheese

2 tablespoons finely sliced fresh chives

1 teaspoon finely chopped fresh rosemary leaves

¼ teaspoon freshly ground black pepper

sea salt, as needed

6 large eggs, at room temperature, yolks and whites separated

1. Preheat the oven to 200°C (400°F) and ensure there is an oven shelf in the centre of the oven. Place a metal baking tray in the oven to heat. Grease six 375 ml (12½ fl oz) capacity ramekins (they need to have straight, vertical sides for the soufflés to rise) and sprinkle with the breadcrumbs.

2. Put the potatoes, garlic and salt in a saucepan and cover with cold water. Bring to the boil over medium–high heat and boil until very tender, about 12 minutes, testing with the point of a sharp knife. Drain the potatoes and return to the saucepan over low heat for 1 minute to ensure any excess water has evaporated. Set the garlic aside.

3. Melt the butter in a small saucepan over medium–low heat. Stir in the anchovies until they almost dissolve into the butter, using the back of the spoon to mash them, about 2 minutes.

4. Mash the potatoes and measure 460 g (1 lb/ 2 cups) into a large mixing bowl. Mash the garlic into the potatoes until very smooth, or pass through a ricer. Pour in the anchovy butter and stir until smooth. Add the buttermilk, parmesan, chives, rosemary and pepper and stir until creamy. Taste and add sea salt and more pepper if needed. Stir the egg yolks into the potato mixture until completely incorporated.

5. In a clean mixing bowl or the bowl of a stand mixer, whisk the egg whites until they are white and stiff, about 2–3 minutes. Using a large metal spoon, gently fold about a quarter of the egg whites into the potato mixture to loosen. Slowly fold through the remaining egg whites until no white streaks remain in the mixture.

6. Divide the mixture among the ramekins. Remove the baking tray from the oven. Place the ramekins on the tray and place on the centre shelf of the oven. Bake until the soufflés are beautifully puffed and golden, about 25–30 minutes. As they cook, admire the rising soufflés through the oven window, but don't open the oven door until near the end of the cooking time.

7. Like all soufflés, these are best served immediately.

souffléd twice-baked potatoes

Crisp on the outside, fluffy on the inside. The perfect baked potato with the usual suspects – sour cream, bacon, cheese, chives – is taken to a new level with a soufflé filling. They look impressive and taste even better. Serve with your favourite salad on the side.

Use floury (starchy or roasting) potatoes; see pages 002–003 for a list of varieties.

4 extra large potatoes, about 1.2 kg (2 lb 10 oz)

2 teaspoons olive oil

1 teaspoon sea salt flakes

30 g (1 oz) unsalted butter

100 g (3½ oz) rindless bacon rashers (slices), diced

1 small garlic clove, finely chopped

2 tablespoons sour cream

50 g (1¾ oz/½ cup) grated parmesan cheese

3 large eggs, at room temperature, whites and yolks separated

1 tablespoon chopped fresh chives, plus extra to serve

½ teaspoon sea salt flakes, plus extra to serve

¼ teaspoon freshly ground black pepper

1. Preheat the oven to 200°C (400°F).

2. Scrub the potatoes and dry them well. Prick with a skewer a few times and rub with the olive oil and sea salt flakes. Place on a tray and bake until tender in the middle when tested with a skewer, about 1 hour.

3. Cut the potatoes in half lengthways and scoop the flesh into a bowl, leaving a rim of about 5 mm–1 cm (¼–½ in) around each potato skin.

4. Return the potato skins to the oven to crisp them, about 10 minutes.

5. Meanwhile, melt the butter in a small frying pan over medium heat. Fry the bacon and the garlic until the bacon is starting to sizzle and the garlic is fragrant, about 4 minutes.

6. In a medium mixing bowl, whisk together the sour cream, parmesan cheese, egg yolks, chives, sea salt and pepper.

7. In a medium mixing bowl, mash the potato flesh until very smooth. Pour the bacon and butter mixture into the potatoes and stir well with a wooden spoon. Add the sour cream mixture and beat until smooth.

8. In a clean mixing bowl or the bowl of a stand mixer, whisk the egg whites until they are white and stiff, about 2–3 minutes. Using a large metal spoon, gently fold about a quarter of the egg whites into the potato mixture to loosen it. Slowly fold through the remaining egg whites until no white streaks remain in the mixture.

9. Divide the mixture among the potato skins and bake until the soufflé potatoes are beautifully puffed and golden, about 30 minutes.

10. Like all soufflés, these are best served immediately, sprinkled with chives and sea salt flakes.

sweet potato soufflés

Sweet potato and Vegemite is a bit of a thing for me (check out the sweet potato macaroni cheese on page 20), but it's such a delicious combination that I can't resist putting them together. Soy sauce is a good alternative as it also delivers a similar salty, umami taste. These soufflés are delicious paired with a salad and some crusty bread on the side.

Use orange sweet potato.

1 large sweet potato, about 600 g (1 lb 5 oz)

3 tablespoons panko (Japanese-style) breadcrumbs

50 g (1¾ oz) unsalted butter

1 garlic clove, finely chopped

3 teaspoons Vegemite, or use soy sauce

190 ml (6½ fl oz/¾ cup) buttermilk

100 g (3½ oz/1 cup) finely grated parmesan cheese

1 tablespoon chopped fresh chives

1 teaspoon finely chopped fresh rosemary leaves

¼ teaspoon freshly ground black pepper

sea salt, to taste

6 large eggs, at room temperature, whites and yolks separated

1. Preheat the oven to 200°C (400°F) and line a baking tray with baking paper.

2. Scrub the sweet potato and pierce it a few times with a skewer. Wrap it in foil, place it on the baking tray and bake until tender, about 55–70 minutes, checking with a skewer. Allow the cooked sweet potato to cool slightly, then peel and process in a food processor until it becomes a smooth purée.

3. Put a metal baking tray in the oven to heat and ensure there is an oven shelf in the centre of the oven. Grease six 375 ml (12½ fl oz/ 1½ cup) capacity ramekins (they need to have straight, vertical sides for the soufflés to rise) and sprinkle with breadcrumbs.

4. Melt the butter in a small saucepan over medium–low heat. Add the garlic and mash with the back of a spoon until almost melted into the butter, about 1 minute. Remove from the heat and stir the Vegemite into the butter until smooth.

5. Measure 500 g (1 lb 2 oz) of the sweet potato purée into a large mixing bowl and stir in the butter mixture, the buttermilk, parmesan, chives, rosemary and pepper until smooth. Taste and add salt and more pepper if needed. Beat in the egg yolks until well combined.

6. In a clean mixing bowl or the bowl of a stand mixer, whisk the egg whites until they are white and stiff, about 2–3 minutes. Using a large metal spoon, gently fold about a quarter of the egg whites into the sweet potato mixture to loosen. Slowly fold through the remaining egg whites until no white streaks remain in the mixture.

7. Divide the mixture among the ramekins. Remove the baking tray from the oven. Place the ramekins on the tray and place on the centre shelf of the oven. Bake until the soufflés are beautifully puffed and golden, about 25–30 minutes. As they cook, admire the rising soufflés through the oven window, but don't open the oven door until near the end of the cooking time.

8. Like all soufflés, these are best served immediately.

spinach, potato and feta pie

You won't be able to stop yourself having a second helping of this pie, with its crispy pastry and delectably creamy filling. If you are using frozen filo pastry, take it out of the freezer and put it in the refrigerator overnight to thaw or leave it on the bench for an hour before you need to use it. Serve the pie with a big green salad.

Use waxy potatoes; see pages 002–003 for a list of varieties.

2 small–medium potatoes, about 280 g (10 oz), peeled and chopped into 1 cm (½ in) cubes

½ teaspoon salt for the cooking water

150 g (5½ oz) unsalted butter, melted, plus extra to grease the baking pan

1 tablespoon olive oil

4 spring onions (scallions), white and green parts sliced, root ends discarded

280 g (10 oz) baby English spinach leaves, roughly chopped

185 g (6½ oz/¾ cup) ricotta cheese

3 large eggs, at room temperature

180 g (6½ oz) feta cheese, drained and chopped into small cubes

50 g (1¾ oz/½ cup) grated parmesan cheese

2 teaspoons chopped fresh dill

¼ teaspoon freshly grated nutmeg

¼ teaspoon freshly ground black pepper

375 g (13 oz) filo pastry (18–20 sheets)

1. Put the potatoes and salt in a small saucepan and cover with cold water. Bring to the boil over medium–high heat and boil until tender, about 8 minutes, testing with the point of a sharp knife. Drain the potatoes and return to the saucepan over low heat for 1 minute to ensure any excess water has evaporated. Set aside to cool.

2. While the potatoes are cooking, preheat the oven to 180°C (350°F). Grease a 30 x 20 x 5 cm (12 x 8 x 2 in) metal baking pan and put a baking tray into the oven to heat.

3. Heat the olive oil in a large frying pan over medium heat. Add the spring onions and cook until they have softened, about 2 minutes. Add a big handful of spinach leaves to the frying pan. As they wilt, add more spinach leaves until all are wilted and tender, about 2–3 minutes. Set aside to cool.

4. In a large mixing bowl, whisk together the ricotta, eggs, feta, parmesan, dill, nutmeg and pepper. Add the spinach mixture and the potatoes and stir until combined.

5. Unwrap the filo pastry and lay it flat on a work surface. As you work, cover the pastry with a sheet of baking paper to prevent it from drying out and becoming brittle.

6. Line the baking pan with 2 sheets of filo pastry. Brush the top sheet of pastry with melted butter. Top with another 2 sheets of filo pastry and again brush the top sheet with melted butter. Repeat until you have used 10 sheets of pastry (5 x 2 sheets). Spoon the spinach and potato mixture into the filo-lined baking pan, spreading it in a flat layer. Take 2 more sheets of filo pastry and cover the filling. Once again, brush the top layer of pastry with melted butter. Repeat until there are no more sheets of pastry left (the top of the pie will have 8–10 sheets of pastry). Fold the overhanging pastry onto the top of the pie and scrunch to form a border around the edge of the pie. Brush with the remaining melted butter. Score the top of the pie into 9 equal pieces with a sharp knife, without cutting all the way through the pastry layers.

7. Put the baking pan on the heated baking tray and bake until golden brown and puffed up, about 50 minutes.

8. Let the pie stand for 10 minutes before cutting along the scored lines to serve.

shepherd's pies

Over-catering seems to be my thing, so there will always be leftovers at my house. Left-over slow-cooked lamb shoulder means shepherd's pies, topped with spring onion mashed potatoes, and always with Vegemite. These are also really good made with minced (ground) lamb. Although these can stand alone as a warming winter meal, you could serve a salad on the side.

Use floury (starchy or roasting) potatoes; see pages 002–003 for a list of varieties.

for the filling

1 tablespoon olive oil

1 large onion, diced

2 celery stalks, sliced

2 large carrots, halved lengthways and sliced

500 g (1 lb 2 oz) diced left-over lamb roast, or minced (ground) lamb

2 tablespoons plain (all-purpose) flour

1 tablespoon tomato paste (concentrated purée)

2 teaspoons Vegemite, or use soy sauce

500 ml (17 fl oz/2 cups) chicken stock (low-salt)

1 tablespoon worcestershire sauce

1 teaspoon fresh thyme leaves

2 bay leaves

½ teaspoon freshly ground black pepper

155 g (5½ oz) frozen peas, or use fresh peas

sea salt

for the topping

6 medium potatoes, about 1 kg (2 lb 3 oz), peeled and chopped into 2 cm (¾ in) pieces

½ teaspoon salt for the cooking water

60 g (2 oz) unsalted butter, melted

½ teaspoon sea salt

¼ teaspoon freshly ground black pepper

125 ml (4 fl oz/½ cup) full-cream (whole) milk

6 spring onions (scallions), white and green parts finely sliced, root ends discarded

25 g (1 oz/¼ cup) grated parmesan cheese

1. Preheat the oven to 200°C (400°F). You will need four 500 ml (17 fl oz/2 cups) capacity ovenproof dishes for the pies.

2. To make the filling, heat the olive oil in a large saucepan over medium heat and cook the onion, stirring occasionally, until soft and lightly golden, about 4 minutes. Add the celery and carrots and cook until softened, stirring occasionally, about 5 minutes. If using left-over lamb, leave the heat at medium and add the lamb. If using minced lamb, increase the heat to medium–high and cook the lamb, breaking it up with a spoon, until lightly browned, about 5 minutes.

3. Sprinkle the flour over the lamb and stir over medium heat for 2 minutes. Stir in the tomato paste and Vegemite until they are absorbed, about 2 minutes. Pour in the stock, worcestershire sauce, thyme, bay leaves and pepper and bring to the boil. Add the peas and stir. Reduce the heat to medium–low and simmer until the sauce has thickened, stirring occasionally, about 20 minutes. Taste and add sea salt and more pepper if needed. Remove the bay leaves and divide the lamb filling between the 4 ovenproof dishes.

4. Put the potatoes and salt in a medium saucepan and cover with cold water. Bring to the boil over medium–high heat and boil until very tender, about 12 minutes, testing with the point of a sharp knife. Drain the potatoes and return to the saucepan over low heat for 1 minute to ensure any excess water has evaporated. Mash well. Using a wooden spoon, stir in the butter, sea salt and pepper and beat until very smooth.

5. Meanwhile, heat the milk and spring onions in a small saucepan over medium heat until the milk is steaming and starting to bubble. Remove from the heat and allow to infuse for 5 minutes before adding to the mashed potatoes. With a wooden spoon, beat until creamy. Taste and add more salt and pepper if needed.

6. Spoon the mash onto the lamb filling in each dish with a light hand, keeping the top rough. Sprinkle the potato with parmesan and bake until the cheesy top is golden and the filling is bubbling, about 25–30 minutes.

7. Stand for 5 minutes before serving, sprinkled with pepper.

scotch egg potato muffins

Part muffin, part Scotch egg, these are popular lunchbox fare for school or work. They're also a great grab-and-go snack on your way out the door.

Use floury (starchy or roasting) potatoes; see pages 002–003 for a list of varieties.

2 small–medium potatoes, about 280 g (10 oz), peeled and chopped into 2 cm (¾ in) cubes

½ teaspoon salt for the cooking water

150 g (5½ oz) rindless bacon rashers (slices), chopped into 1.5 cm (½ in) pieces

225 g (8 oz/1½ cups) plain (all-purpose) flour

2 teaspoons baking powder

250 ml (8½ fl oz/1 cup) buttermilk, at room temperature

2 large eggs, at room temperature

125 g (4½ oz/1 cup) grated cheddar cheese

2 tablespoons finely sliced fresh chives

¼ teaspoon sea salt

¼ teaspoon black pepper

6 small eggs, soft-boiled and shelled

1½ tablespoons grated parmesan cheese

1. Preheat the oven to 180°C (350°F). Line a baking tray with baking paper. Line each hole of a 6-hole Texas muffin pan with baking paper or large paper cases.

2. Put the potatoes and salt in a small saucepan and cover with cold water. Bring to the boil over medium–high heat and boil until very tender, about 12 minutes, testing with the point of a sharp knife. Drain the potatoes and return to the saucepan over low heat for 1 minute to ensure any excess water has evaporated. Put the potato through a ricer or mash well until very smooth. Set aside to cool to room temperature.

3. Meanwhile, place the bacon on the baking tray and bake until sizzling and golden, about 10–12 minutes. Set aside to cool.

4. In a medium mixing bowl, combine the flour and baking powder.

5. Measure 230 g (8 oz/1 cup) of mashed potato into a large mixing bowl. Add 60 ml (2 fl oz/¼ cup) of buttermilk and stir until smooth. Add the remaining buttermilk to the potato and stir until creamy. Add the eggs, one at a time, and stir until completely incorporated. Stir in the bacon, cheddar, chives, the sea salt and pepper. Add the flour mixture and stir until just combined.

6. Put 1 heaped tablespoon of the batter into each muffin cup. Sit a boiled egg, fat end down, on top of the batter. Carefully spoon the remaining batter around and on top of each egg, ensuring the egg is completely covered with batter. Sprinkle each muffin with 1 teaspoon of grated parmesan.

7. Bake in the oven until the cheese on each muffin is golden, about 25 minutes. The top of the muffin should bounce back when gently pressed. Put the muffin pan on a wire rack for 5 minutes, then transfer each muffin to the wire rack to cool.

8. Store the muffins in the refrigerator in an airtight container for up to 3 days.

balsamic chicken and potatoes

A simple dish with few ingredients that ticks all the boxes for a tasty, easy meal. It's perfect for a lazy night in. It's delicious with steamed broccoli on the side.

Use new potatoes.

1 kg (2 lb 3 oz) chicken thighs, skin on and bone in

600 g (1 lb 5 oz) new potatoes, halved

8 garlic cloves, peeled and left whole

60 ml (2 fl oz/¼ cup) olive oil

1 tablespoon balsamic vinegar

2 teaspoons fresh thyme leaves, plus extra to serve

1 teaspoon sea salt

¼ teaspoon freshly ground black pepper

2 small lemons, scrubbed and cut in half

1. Preheat the oven to 200°C (400°F). You need a large baking pan, about 35 x 25 x 5 cm (13¾ x 10 x 2 in).

2. Trim the chicken thighs of excess fat and place them in the baking pan with the potatoes and the garlic cloves.

3. In a small mixing bowl, whisk together the oil, balsamic vinegar, thyme, sea salt and pepper until the oil and vinegar are emulsified. Pour this over the chicken and potatoes and toss everything together until well coated in the balsamic mixture. Ensure the chicken is in a single layer, skin side up, nestled among the potatoes. Squeeze some of the juice from the lemon halves over the chicken and potatoes, then place the lemon halves in the pan.

4. Bake for 50 minutes or until the potatoes are tender and the chicken pieces are cooked through (the juices should run clear when pierced with a skewer, with no trace of pink). Halfway through the cooking time, baste the chicken and the potatoes with the pan juices. Turn the chicken if the skin is becoming too dark.

5. To serve, sprinkle with thyme.

spelt and potato pizza

This pizza has the total wow factor. Potatoes and rosemary are always a winning combination, and cheese is a given. Then there's bacon and onion jam, which lifts this pizza to knockout. For an added punch of flavour, throw on some sliced olives.

Use waxy potatoes; see pages 002–003 for a list of varieties.

for the bacon and onion jam

350 g (12½ oz) rindless streaky bacon, cut into 1 cm (½ in) pieces

30 g (1 oz) unsalted butter

2 large onions, about 400 g (14 oz), quartered and thinly sliced

125 ml (4 fl oz/½ cup) cold brewed coffee

2 tablespoons maple syrup

2 tablespoons balsamic vinegar

1 large granny smith apple or other tart cooking apple, peeled, cored and grated

1 teaspoon fresh thyme leaves

¼ teaspoon freshly ground black pepper

for the pizza

250 ml (8½ fl oz/1 cup) lukewarm water, about 40–42°C (104–108°F)

1 teaspoon honey

2¼ teaspoons dry yeast, about 7 g (¼ oz)

210 g (7½ oz/1½ cups) white spelt flour

225 g (8 oz/1½ cups) plain (all-purpose) flour

2 teaspoons sea salt

60 ml (2 fl oz/¼ cup) full-cream (whole) milk

60 ml (2 fl oz/¼ cup) olive oil

3 small potatoes, about 300 g (10½ oz)

½ teaspoon salt for the cooking water

225 g (8 oz/1½ cups) grated mozzarella cheese

1 teaspoon chopped fresh rosemary, plus extra to serve

25 g (1 oz/¼ cup) grated parmesan cheese

1. In a large frying pan over medium heat, cook the bacon until golden, stirring occasionally, about 20 minutes. Transfer the bacon to a plate lined with paper towel. (Don't wash or scrape out the frying pan.)

2. In the same frying pan, melt the butter and cook the onions, stirring occasionally and scraping up any brown bits at the bottom of the frying pan, until there are touches of gold on the onion slices, about 4 minutes. Reduce the heat to medium–low, cooking the onions until they are very soft and golden, about 20 minutes.

3. Return the bacon to the pan and stir in the coffee, maple syrup, balsamic vinegar, apple, thyme and pepper. Cook until reduced and thickened, about 40–50 minutes, stirring occasionally.

4. To make the pizza dough, pour the lukewarm water into a small measuring jug. Stir in the honey. Sprinkle the yeast over the water and stir gently. Set aside until the top of the water is foamy, about 5–10 minutes.

Recipe continues on next page.

spelt and potato pizza (continued)

5. In a large mixing bowl or the bowl of a stand mixer, whisk together the flours and sea salt. Stir in the yeast and water mixture, milk and 2 tablespoons of the olive oil.

6. If using a stand mixer, insert the dough hook and knead until the dough is smooth and still slightly sticky, about 4 minutes. Alternatively, turn the dough onto a lightly floured work surface and knead until smooth and still slightly sticky, about 4 minutes. Shape the dough into a ball.

7. Oil a large mixing bowl with 1 teaspoon of olive oil. Put the dough in the bowl and cover with plastic wrap. Set aside in a warm place until doubled in size, about 30–40 minutes.

8. Preheat the oven to 230°C (450°F) and line 2 baking trays with baking paper.

9. Meanwhile, scrub the potatoes (peel if you like) and cut them into 3 mm (⅛ in) slices. Put the potato slices and the salt in a small saucepan and cover with cold water. Bring to the boil over medium–high heat and boil until not quite tender, about 3–4 minutes. Drain the potatoes and dry them on paper towel.

10. Turn the dough onto a lightly floured work surface and divide into 2 pieces. Roll each piece of dough into a rough rectangle to fit on a baking tray, about 30 x 20 cm (12 x 8 in).

11. Spread each pizza with about 1 cup of bacon and onion jam, then sprinkle with mozzarella and layer with potato slices. Drizzle with the remaining olive oil and sprinkle half of the rosemary over the potatoes on each pizza. Bake until the base is golden and the potatoes are cooked, about 20 minutes.

12. Sprinkle with the parmesan and additional rosemary, and slice to serve.

spiced lamb with potatoes, capsicum and tomatoes

I love to make this dish on a lazy Sunday afternoon. With everything in one baking dish it doesn't take long to prepare, and then you just pop it in the oven. By dinnertime the house smells so heavenly that everyone will be hanging around the kitchen, waiting to eat. Serve with bread on the side.

Use waxy or new potatoes; see pages 002–003 for a list of varieties.

4 medium–large potatoes, about 750 g (1 lb 11 oz), or use new potatoes

2 large red onions, halved and sliced into slim wedges

80 ml (2½ fl oz/⅓ cup) olive oil

1 large garlic clove, finely chopped

1 teaspoon ground coriander

1 teaspoon ground cumin

1 teaspoon grated lemon zest

1 teaspoon sea salt

½ teaspoon freshly ground black pepper

1 kg (2 lb 3 oz) lamb shoulder, boned

2 red capsicums (bell peppers), seeded and chopped into 2 cm (¾ in) pieces

5 smallish tomatoes, about 350 g (12½ oz), cored and quartered

170 ml (5½ fl oz/⅔ cup) chicken stock (low-salt)

1 tablespoon lemon juice

10 g (¼ oz/⅓ cup) chopped fresh flat-leaf (Italian) parsley, plus extra to serve

1. Preheat the oven to 180°C (350°F). You need a large baking pan, about 35 x 25 x 5 cm (13¾ x 10 x 2 in).

2. Peel the potatoes and slice into quarters lengthways, then chop each long quarter in half. If using new potatoes, halve them. Add the onions and potatoes to the baking pan with the oil, garlic, coriander, cumin, lemon zest, sea salt and pepper. Stir well. Lean in and smell the deliciously fragrant combination of spices.

3. Trim the lamb of most of the outer layer of fat and chop into 3 cm (1¼ in) cubes. Add to the baking pan and toss well to coat in the oil and spices. Add the capsicum and tomatoes to the baking pan, pour over the chicken stock and lemon juice and stir it all together.

4. Cover the baking pan tightly with foil or with a lid and bake for 2 hours. Remove from the oven to stir halfway through the cooking time.

5. Increase the oven temperature to 200°C (400°F). Remove the baking pan from the oven and take off the foil or lid. Stir through the parsley. Taste and add more sea salt if needed. Stirring occasionally, bake until the liquid has reduced and the potatoes and lamb are golden, about a further 45 minutes to 1 hour.

6. Serve in wide, shallow bowls, sprinkled with parsley.

fry

potato, chorizo and beef empanadas

Wrapped in pastry and deep-fried, these are the perfect snack on a cold day – or, really, any time. If you want some heat, serve them with your favourite hot sauce.

Use floury (starchy or roasting) potatoes; see pages 002–003 for a list of varieties.

for the filling

2 small potatoes, about 200 g (7 oz), peeled and cut into 2 cm (¾ in) cubes

¼ teaspoon salt for the cooking water

1 tablespoon olive oil

150 g (5½ oz) minced (ground) beef

125 g (4½ oz) chorizo, quartered lengthways and sliced

½ small onion, diced

2 garlic cloves, finely diced

1 teaspoon dried oregano

½ teaspoon ground cumin

125 ml (4 fl oz/½ cup) chicken stock (low-salt)

50 g (1¾ oz/⅓ cup) frozen peas, or use fresh peas

1 hard-boiled egg, diced

for the dough

450 g (1 lb/3 cups) plain (all-purpose) flour

1 teaspoon baking powder

1 teaspoon sea salt

125 g (4½ oz) unsalted butter, melted

250 ml (8½ fl oz/1 cup) warm water

for frying

up to 2 litres (68 fl oz/8 cups) vegetable oil

1. Put the potatoes and salt in a small saucepan and cover with cold water. Bring to the boil and simmer until tender, about 10–12 minutes, testing with the point of a sharp knife.

2. Meanwhile, for the filling, heat the olive oil in a frying pan over medium–high heat and brown the beef and chorizo, stirring often to break up any lumps of minced beef, about 4 minutes. Reduce the heat to medium, add the onion and cook until soft, stirring occasionally, about 3 minutes. Add the garlic, oregano and cumin and cook until the garlic is soft and the spices are fragrant, stirring occasionally, about 2 minutes. Pour in the chicken stock and add the potatoes, roughly mashing them with a fork. Add the peas and bring to the boil. Simmer until the peas are cooked and most of the liquid has evaporated, about 3 minutes. Remove from the heat and add the hard-boiled egg. Set the filling aside to cool completely.

3. To make the dough, combine the flour, baking powder and sea salt together in a mixing bowl. Pour in the butter and mix with a fork until it looks like breadcrumbs. Add the warm water, a little at a time, until the dough holds together but is not too sticky. You may not need all of the water. Turn the dough onto a lightly floured work surface and knead until smooth and elastic, about 3 minutes. Form a disc, cover with plastic wrap and rest in the refrigerator for 30 minutes.

4. Divide the dough into 12 even pieces and roll each piece into a ball with your hands. On a lightly floured work surface, roll each piece of dough into a 15 cm (6 in) circle, about 2–3 mm (¹⁄₁₆–⅛ in) thick. If you don't have a thermometer, keep a small piece of dough aside to test when the oil is ready for frying.

Recipe continues on next page.

potato, chorizo and
beef empanadas (continued)

5. Divide the filling into 12 portions. Place a portion of filling on one side of each dough circle. Lightly brush the edges of each circle with cold water, fold the dough over and press the edges together with your fingers to form a half circle. Using your fingers, twist the edges of the empanadas to seal. Chill the empanadas in the refrigerator, uncovered, for 30–60 minutes.

6. Pour the vegetable oil into a large, deep pot to a depth of about 7 cm (2¾ in). Heat the oil over medium–high heat until it is about 180°C (350°F). If you don't have a thermometer, carefully lower a piece of the pastry into the oil to test if it's ready. If the oil bubbles around the pastry and the pastry rises quickly to the surface of the oil, it's ready to use. Fry 3–4 empanadas at a time, turning once, until golden on both sides, about 5 minutes in total. Transfer the empanadas to a wire rack lined with paper towel. If the temperature of the oil keeps increasing or it starts to smoke, reduce the heat to medium.

7. Allow the empanadas to cool for 2 minutes before serving.

duck fat potato fritters

Take your breakfast upmarket with these duck fat potato fritters. To make things easy in the morning, the fritters can be made the night before, stored in the refrigerator and reheated in a 190°C (375°F) oven until crisp. Perfect.

Use floury (starchy or roasting) potatoes; see pages 002–003 for a list of varieties.

1 teaspoon lemon juice

3 medium potatoes, about 500 g (1 lb 2 oz)

35 g (1¼ oz/¼ cup) plain (all-purpose) flour

40 g (1½ oz/¼ cup) potato starch, or substitute 35 g (1¼ oz/¼ cup) plain (all-purpose) flour

2 teaspoons fresh thyme leaves

1 teaspoon sea salt

½ teaspoon freshly ground black pepper

1 large egg, whisked

80–160 ml (2½–5½ fl oz/⅓–⅔ cup) rendered duck fat, as needed

to serve

sea salt flakes

125 g (4½ oz/½ cup) sour cream

1. Add the lemon juice and 500 ml (17 fl oz/ 2 cups) cold water to a large mixing bowl.

2. Peel the potatoes and cut them into thin matchsticks. Drop the potato pieces into the water and set aside for 30 minutes. Drain into a mesh strainer and rinse under running water. Place the potatoes in the centre of a clean tea towel (dish towel), folding and twisting it into a ball. Squeeze over the sink to drain off as much liquid as possible.

3. In a large mixing bowl, whisk together the flour, potato starch, thyme, salt and pepper. Add the potatoes and mix until the flour is absorbed. Add the egg and mix until well incorporated.

4. Preheat the oven to 160°C (320°F) and line a baking tray with baking paper.

5. Heat 80 ml (2½ fl oz/⅓ cup) of the duck fat in a frying pan over medium–high heat. Drop tablespoons of batter into the oil and flatten slightly with the back of the spoon. They should sizzle immediately. Fry about 4 fritters at a time, leaving plenty of room around each one. Cook until the edges of the fritters are golden and crisp, about 3–4 minutes. Turn and cook for a further 3–4 minutes. If the duck fat starts to smoke, reduce the heat to medium. Repeat with the rest of the potato mixture, adding more duck fat as needed to maintain a 3–4 mm (⅛ in) layer in the pan.

6. Transfer the cooked fritters to a plate lined with paper towel to soak up any excess oil, then transfer to the baking tray and place in the oven to keep them hot while you make the rest of the fritters.

7. Serve sprinkled with sea salt flakes and pepper, with sour cream on the side.

potato doughnuts

Mashed potatoes make these doughnuts so soft and fluffy they may even convert non-doughnut lovers.

Use floury (starchy or roasting) potatoes; see pages 002–003 for a list of varieties.

for the doughnuts

3 medium potatoes, about 500 g (1 lb 2 oz), peeled and cut into 2.5 cm (1 in) pieces

2 large eggs, at room temperature, whisked

600 g (1 lb 5 oz/4 cups) plain (all-purpose) flour

145 g (5 oz/⅔ cup) caster (superfine) sugar

3 teaspoons baking powder

1 teaspoon sea salt

60 g (2 oz) unsalted butter, melted

250 ml (8½ fl oz/1 cup) buttermilk, at room temperature

1 teaspoon natural vanilla extract

for the cinnamon sugar

230 g (8 oz/1 cup) caster (superfine) sugar

2 teaspoons ground cinnamon

for frying

up to 2 litres (68 fl oz/8 cups) vegetable oil

1. Put the potatoes in a saucepan and cover with cold water. Bring to the boil over medium–high heat and boil until very tender, about 15 minutes, testing with the point of a sharp knife. Drain the potatoes and return to the saucepan over low heat for 1 minute to ensure any excess water has evaporated. Put the potatoes through a ricer or mash thoroughly until very smooth.

2. In a large mixing bowl, whisk together the flour, sugar, baking powder and sea salt.

3. Measure 460 g (1 lb/2 cups) of potato into a large mixing bowl. Add the melted butter and stir with a wooden spoon until smooth. Add the buttermilk and vanilla and beat until creamy. Add the eggs and stir until they are completely incorporated. Fold in the flour mixture until just combined. Cover the bowl with plastic wrap and rest the dough in the refrigerator for 2 hours or overnight.

4. Line 2 baking trays with baking paper. On a lightly floured work surface, knead the dough until smooth, about 1 minute. If the dough is quite sticky, knead in extra flour, a tablespoon at a time. Roll out the dough until it is 1.5–2 cm (½–¾ in) thick. If you don't have a thermometer, keep a small piece of dough aside to test when the oil is ready. Use a doughnut cutter to cut out the doughnuts, then place them on the trays. If you don't have a doughnut cutter, use a large cookie cutter for the outside of the doughnut and a very

small cookie cutter or sharp knife to cut the doughnut hole. Set them aside in the refrigerator, uncovered, for 45 minutes.

5. To make the cinnamon sugar, combine the sugar and cinnamon in a wide, shallow bowl. Set aside.

6. Pour the vegetable oil into a large, deep pot to a depth of about 7 cm (2¾ in). Heat the oil over medium–high heat until 180°C (350°F). If you don't have a thermometer, carefully lower a piece of the dough into the oil to test if it's ready. If the oil bubbles around the dough and the dough rises quickly to the surface of the oil, it's ready to use. Fry 3–4 doughnuts at a time until golden, turning once, about 3 minutes in total. Transfer the doughnuts to a wire rack lined with paper towel. If the temperature of the oil continues to rise or starts to smoke, reduce the heat to medium.

7. After the doughnuts have cooled for about 30 seconds, roll them in the cinnamon sugar and serve immediately.

chorizo potato balls

These seem to disappear as soon as I put them on a wire rack to cool! Fried potato is always delicious, but these are especially so; the potato is fluffy and light, studded with chorizo and chives. They make excellent finger food for a party.

Use floury (starchy or roasting) potatoes; see pages 002–003 for a list of varieties.

3 medium potatoes, about 500 g (1 lb 2 oz), peeled and cut into 2.5 cm (1 in) pieces

1 garlic clove, peeled and left whole

½ teaspoon salt for the cooking water

30 g (1 oz) unsalted butter, melted

1 teaspoon olive oil

250–280 g (9–10 oz) chorizo, quartered lengthways and thinly sliced

2 tablespoons finely sliced fresh chives

1 large egg, at room temperature, whisked

75 g (2¾ oz/½ cup) plain (all-purpose) flour

½ teaspoon baking powder

up to 2 litres (68 fl oz/8 cups) vegetable oil

1. Put the potatoes, garlic and salt in a small saucepan and cover with cold water. Bring to the boil over medium–high heat and boil until very tender, about 15 minutes, testing with the point of a sharp knife. Drain the potatoes and garlic and return them to the saucepan over low heat for 1 minute to ensure any excess water has evaporated. Set the garlic aside.

2. Mash the potatoes and measure 460 g (1 lb/2 cups) into a large mixing bowl. Add the garlic and mash thoroughly with the potatoes until very smooth, or pass the potatoes and garlic through a ricer. Pour in the butter and beat with a wooden spoon until smooth.

3. Meanwhile, heat the olive oil in a medium frying pan over medium heat and cook the chorizo until golden and crisp, about 5 minutes. Tip the chorizo and any oil from the frying pan into the potato along with the chives and stir until combined. Add the egg to the potato and stir until well combined.

4. Whisk together the flour and baking powder in a small mixing bowl. Stir them into the potato until just combined. Cover the bowl with plastic wrap and place in the refrigerator for 1 hour.

5. Line a baking tray with baking paper. Using a small cookie dough scoop or a tablespoon, place balls of the dough on the baking tray, ready to fry.

6. Pour the vegetable oil into a large, deep pot to a depth of about 7 cm (2¾ in). Heat the oil over medium–high heat until 180°C (350°F). If you don't have a thermometer, carefully lower a piece of the dough into the oil to test if it's ready. If the oil bubbles around the dough and the dough rises quickly to the surface of the oil, it's ready to use. Fry 6–8 chorizo potato balls at a time, turning once, about 4 minutes until golden and cooked. Transfer the chorizo potato balls to a wire rack lined with paper towel. If the temperature of the oil continues to rise or starts to smoke, reduce the heat to medium.

7. Serve the potato balls as they are or with your favourite dipping sauce.

ultimate grilled cheese sandwich

Of course there's cheese – that's a given. But there are also thin slices of stacked potato and, quite frankly, an awesome bacon and onion jam. Butter the outside of the bread and cook these in a frying pan, or use a sandwich press if you have one. The jam recipe makes oodles, and is also used in the spelt and potato pizza (page 82).

Use waxy (boiling) potatoes; see pages 002–003 for a list of varieties.

for the bacon and onion jam

350 g (12½ oz) rindless streaky bacon, cut into 1 cm (½ in) pieces

30 g (1 oz) unsalted butter

2 large onions, about 400 g (14 oz), quartered and thinly sliced

125 ml (4 fl oz/½ cup) cold brewed coffee

2 tablespoons maple syrup

2 tablespoons balsamic vinegar

1 large granny smith apple or other tart cooking apple, peeled, cored and grated

1 teaspoon fresh thyme leaves

¼ teaspoon freshly ground black pepper

for the sandwiches

4 small potatoes, about 400 g (14 oz), or use left-over potato gratin or roast potatoes

¼ teaspoon salt for the cooking water

8 slices of bread (use dark rye, sourdough or whatever you prefer)

60 g (2 oz/¼ cup) sour cream

150 g (5½ oz) brie, sliced, or use jarlsberg, gruyère or cheddar cheese if you prefer

freshly ground black pepper

60 g (2 oz) unsalted butter

to serve

sea salt flakes

1. In a large frying pan over medium heat, cook the bacon until starting to brown, about 20 minutes. Transfer the bacon to a plate lined with paper towel. (Don't wash or scrape out the frying pan.)

2. In the same frying pan, melt the butter and cook the onions, stirring occasionally and scraping up any brown bits at the bottom of the frying pan, until there are touches of gold on the onion slices, about 4 minutes. Reduce the heat to medium–low, cooking the onions until they are very soft and golden, about 20 minutes.

3. Return the bacon to the pan and stir in the coffee, maple syrup, balsamic vinegar, apple, thyme and pepper. Cook until reduced and thickened, about 40–50 minutes, stirring occasionally.

4. Scrub the potatoes (peel them if you like) and slice into 3 mm (⅛ in) slices. Put the potatoes and salt in a small saucepan and cover with cold water. Bring to the boil over medium–high heat and boil until tender, about 5 minutes. Drain the potatoes and dry them on paper towel. Alternatively, slice left-over roast potatoes or use left-over potato gratin for the sandwiches.

5. Take 2 slices of bread and spread a teaspoon of sour cream on each slice. On one slice, on top of the sour cream, spread 1–2 tablespoons bacon and onion jam. Next, layer about a quarter of the potato slices on the bacon and onion jam and top with a quarter of the sliced brie or cheese of your choice. Sprinkle with pepper. Place the second piece of bread on top of the sandwich, sour cream side down. Butter the outside of the bread slices. Repeat for the remaining sandwiches.

6. Heat a medium frying pan over medium heat. Place 2 sandwiches in the frying pan, butter side down, and cook until they are nicely browned underneath, about 4 minutes. Turn and cook for a further 4 minutes, pressing down on the sandwiches with a spatula a couple of times. You're aiming for toasted outside and melting cheese inside the sandwich. Repeat with the remaining sandwiches. Alternatively, the sandwiches can be cooked in a sandwich press.

7. Sprinkle the sandwiches with sea salt flakes and serve with a glass of milk or a nice frothy milkshake. Two straws, of course.

spelt sweet potato pancakes

Fluffy, golden sweet potato pancakes. Stack them high, drizzle with maple syrup and add a sprinkle of pecans for an impressive breakfast that will be requested often.

Use an orange sweet potato.

1 medium–large sweet potato, about
 420 g (15 oz)

140 g (5 oz) white spelt flour, or use plain
 (all-purpose) flour

2 teaspoons baking powder

1 teaspoon sea salt

½ teaspoon ground cinnamon

¼ teaspoon freshly grated nutmeg

60 g (2 oz) unsalted butter, plus extra for frying

250 ml (8½ fl oz/1 cup) buttermilk

165 ml (5½ fl oz/¾ cup) pure maple syrup

2 large eggs, at room temperature

½ teaspoon grated orange zest

to serve

30 g (1 oz/¼ cup) chopped pecans or walnuts

1. Preheat the oven to 200°C (400°F) and line a baking tray with baking paper.

2. Scrub the sweet potato and pierce it a few times with a skewer. Wrap it in foil, place on the baking tray and bake until completely tender, about 60–70 minutes, checking with a skewer. Allow the cooked sweet potato to cool slightly, then peel and put it through a ricer or mash well until very smooth.

3. In a medium mixing bowl, whisk together the flour, baking powder, sea salt, cinnamon and nutmeg.

4. In a small saucepan over medium heat, melt the butter. Remove it from the heat and whisk in the buttermilk, 2 tablespoons of maple syrup, the eggs and orange zest.

5. Measure 375 g (13 oz/1½ cups) of mashed sweet potato into a large mixing bowl. Pour half of the buttermilk mixture over the sweet potato and mix well with a wooden spoon. Add the remaining buttermilk mixture and beat until smooth. Add the flour and stir until just combined. Place the batter in the refrigerator for 30 minutes.

6. Melt 2 teaspoons of butter in a large frying pan over medium heat and swirl to coat the bottom of the pan. Pour about 60 ml (2 fl oz/ ¼ cup) of batter per pancake into the hot frying pan, cooking 3–4 pancakes at a time. Turn the pancakes when the edges look set, about 3 minutes. Cook for a further 2–3 minutes on the other side, then transfer to a serving plate. Repeat with the remaining batter, adding more butter to the frying pan if needed.

7. Serve the pancakes drizzled with maple syrup and sprinkled with pecans.

curried potato cakes

I like to prepare these potato cakes the night before and leave them, covered, in the refrigerator so the next day dinner is super easy to cook. You could serve them with a tomato salad on the side or they make a yummy vegetarian burger with spinach leaves and tomato chutney on a soft roll.

Use floury (starchy or roasting) potatoes; see pages 002–003 for a list of varieties.

2 medium–large potatoes, about 550 g (1 lb 3 oz), peeled and cut into 3 cm (1¼ in) pieces

¼ teaspoon salt for the cooking water

¼ teaspoon sea salt

½ teaspoon freshly ground black pepper

2 teaspoons curry powder

100 g (3½ oz/⅔ cup) frozen peas

90 g (3 oz/1½ cups) panko (Japanese-style) breadcrumbs

2 large eggs, at room temperature, whisked

1 tablespoon sliced fresh chives

80 ml (2½ fl oz/⅓ cup) olive oil

1. Put the potatoes and salt in a medium saucepan and cover with cold water. Bring to the boil over medium–high heat and boil until very tender, about 15 minutes, testing with the point of a sharp knife. Drain the potatoes and return to the saucepan over low heat for 1 minute to ensure any excess water has evaporated. Mash the potatoes well and transfer to a medium mixing bowl.

2. Add the sea salt, pepper and curry powder and stir until the potato is golden.

3. Cook the peas according to the packet instructions, drain and stir them through the potato mixture.

4. Stir one-third of the panko breadcrumbs into the potato mixture, then stir through the beaten eggs until you can no longer see streaks of egg.

5. Place the remaining panko breadcrumbs in a wide, shallow dish. Divide the potato mixture equally into 12 balls and form each into a round patty 1.5 cm (½ in) deep. If you'll be making burgers, divide the mixture into 6 balls and form them into round patties about 2 cm (¾ in) thick. Place each patty in the panko breadcrumbs and turn to coat. Place each patty on the plate, cover and refrigerate for at least 1 hour or overnight.

6. When ready to cook the potato cakes, preheat the oven to 160°C (320°F) and line a baking tray with baking paper.

7. Heat 2 tablespoons of olive oil in a large frying pan over medium heat. Cook 6 potato cakes until the bottoms are brown and crispy, about 5 minutes. If making burgers, cook 3 large potato patties at a time. Turn them carefully and cook for a further 5 minutes on the other side. Transfer the cooked potato cakes/patties to the baking tray and place them in the oven to keep warm. Pour the remaining olive oil into the pan and cook the remaining potato cakes/patties in the same way.

8. Serve immediately as the centre of a main meal or the star of a vegetarian burger.

new French toast

Change up sweet French toast and add a touch of excitement to breakfast with this new version made with slices of potato and chorizo loaf (page 137). It's particularly yummy with creamy scrambled eggs.

6 large eggs, at room temperature

375 ml (12½ fl oz/1½ cups) full-cream (whole) milk

½ teaspoon sea salt

¼ teaspoon freshly ground black pepper

Potato and chorizo loaf (page 137), made the day before

80 ml (2½ fl oz/⅓ cup) olive oil

120 g (4½ oz) unsalted butter

to serve

2 tablespoons chopped fresh flat-leaf (Italian) parsley

freshly ground black pepper

1. Preheat the oven to 160°C (320°F) and line a baking tray with baking paper.

2. Whiz the eggs, milk, sea salt and pepper together in a blender until smooth (or whisk in a medium mixing bowl until smooth).

3. Slice the potato and chorizo loaf into 2.5 cm (1 in) slices (about 12 slices in total). Reserve 6 of the slices.

4. Put 6 of the loaf slices in a large dish in a single layer and pour over half of the egg mixture. Soak for 5 minutes and then turn the slices over and soak for a further 5 minutes.

5. Heat 1 tablespoon of olive oil and 30 g (1 oz) of butter in a large frying pan over medium–high heat. Fry 3 of the egg-soaked slices until golden, about 3–4 minutes on each side. Place them on the baking tray and keep them warm in the oven. Add 1 tablespoon of oil and 30 g (1 oz) butter to the frying pan and fry the remaining 3 egg-soaked slices. Place them on the baking tray and keep them warm in the oven.

6. Meanwhile, put the remaining 6 slices of potato and chorizo loaf into the dish and cover with the remaining egg mixture. Soak for 5 minutes and then turn the slices over and soak for a further 5 minutes. Cook as for the first 6 slices.

7. Serve sprinkled with parsley and pepper.

potato, apple and parmesan fritters

I always find myself pinching one or two of these delightfully crisp little fritters almost straight from the pan. But save a few, if you can, as they are perfect for a lazy brunch with poached eggs and crispy bacon.

Use floury (starchy or roasting) potatoes; see pages 002–003 for a list of varieties.

1 teaspoon lemon juice

3 medium potatoes, about 500 g (1 lb 2 oz)

2 large granny smith apples or other tart cooking apples

50 g (1¾ oz/1 cup) grated parmesan cheese

35 g (1¼ oz/¼ cup) plain (all-purpose) flour

40 g (1½ oz/¼ cup) potato starch, or substitute 35 g (1¼ oz/¼ cup) plain (all-purpose) flour

2 tablespoons sliced fresh chives, plus extra to serve

1 teaspoon fresh thyme leaves

1 teaspoon sea salt

½ teaspoon freshly ground black pepper, plus extra to serve

1 large egg, whisked

80–160 ml (2½–5½ fl oz/⅓–⅔ cup) vegetable oil, as needed

to serve

sea salt flakes

125 g (4½ oz/½ cup) sour cream

1. Add the lemon juice and 500 ml (17 fl oz/ 2 cups) cold water to a mixing bowl.

2. Peel the potatoes and grate them on the largest holes of your grater. Drop the grated potato straight into the water as you grate each potato. Peel and grate the apples and drop the grated apple into the water as you grate each apple. Give the water a swirl to mix the potato and apple and set aside for 30 minutes. Drain into a mesh strainer and rinse under running water. Drop the grated potato and apple into the centre of a clean tea towel (dish towel), folding and twisting it into a ball. Squeeze over the sink to drain off as much liquid as possible.

3. In a large mixing bowl, whisk together the parmesan, flour, potato starch, chives, thyme, sea salt and pepper. Add the grated potato and apple and mix until the flour is absorbed. Add the egg and mix until well incorporated.

4. Preheat the oven to 160°C (320°F) and line a baking tray with baking paper.

5. Heat 80 ml (2½ fl oz/⅓ cup) of the vegetable oil in a frying pan over medium–high heat. Drop tablespoons of batter into the oil and flatten slightly with the back of the spoon. Fry about 4 fritters at a time, leaving plenty of room around each one. Cook until the edges of the fritters are golden and crisp, about 3–4 minutes. Turn and cook for a further 3–4 minutes. If the oil starts to smoke, reduce the heat to medium.

6. Transfer the cooked fritters to a plate lined with paper towel to soak up any excess oil, then transfer to the baking tray and place in the oven to keep them hot while you make the rest of the fritters.

7. Repeat with the rest of the potato mixture, adding more vegetable oil as needed to maintain a 3–4 mm (⅛ in) layer of vegetable oil in the pan.

8. Serve sprinkled with sea salt flakes, pepper and chives, with sour cream on the side.

chill

potato, pea and mint salad

Potatoes and peas are two humble vegetables that work so well together in this lovely salad. The sweetness of maple syrup in the dressing adds a flavour that you don't often get with potato – but trust me, it's fresh and delicious.

Use new potatoes.

for the salad

1 kg (2 lb 3 oz) new potatoes, scrubbed

½ teaspoon salt for the cooking water

155 g (5½ oz/1 cup) frozen peas, or use fresh peas

for the dressing

125 ml (4 fl oz/½ cup) olive oil

2 tablespoons red wine vinegar

2 teaspoons maple syrup

½ teaspoon sea salt

¼ teaspoon freshly ground black pepper, plus extra to serve

4 tablespoons finely chopped fresh chives

4 tablespoons finely sliced fresh mint leaves, plus extra to serve

to serve

2 large eggs, hard-boiled and sliced

2 tablespoons chopped walnuts

1. Put the potatoes and salt in a medium saucepan and cover with cold water. Bring to the boil over medium–high heat and boil until not quite tender, about 12–15 minutes, testing with the point of a sharp knife. Add the peas and cook for a further 3 minutes, until the peas and potatoes are cooked and tender. Drain the potatoes and peas and refresh them under cold running water. Drain again and set aside to cool.

2. To make the dressing, whisk together the olive oil, vinegar, maple syrup, sea salt and pepper until emulsified. Stir in the chives and mint.

3. To make the salad, cut the potatoes into 1 cm (½ in) slices and put them in a large mixing bowl with the peas. Pour in the dressing and toss to combine.

4. To serve, transfer the salad to a serving dish and garnish with the eggs, walnuts, mint leaves and pepper.

5. Store in the refrigerator until ready to serve. This salad is best eaten on the day it is made.

sweet potato and rice salad with orange cumin dressing

Perfect on a hot summer day, this salad pairs beautifully with lamb or other barbecued meat.

Use orange sweet potatoes.

for the salad

1 large sweet potato, about 650 g (1 lb 7 oz), chopped into 2 cm (¾ in) pieces

1 medium red capsicum (bell pepper), seeded and chopped into 2 cm (¾ in) pieces

1 medium red onion, chopped into wedges

1 tablespoon olive oil

1 teaspoon ground cumin

½ teaspoon salt

60 g (2 oz/½ cup) chopped walnuts

100 g (3½ oz/½ cup) uncooked long-grain rice

80 g (2¾ oz) feta cheese, diced

55 g (2 oz/⅓ cup) dried cranberries

2 celery stalks, halved lengthways and sliced

10 g (¼ oz/⅓ cup) chopped celery leaves, or use flat-leaf (Italian) parsley

for the dressing

80 ml (2½ fl oz/⅓ cup) freshly squeezed orange juice

2 teaspoons orange zest

2 teaspoons honey, warmed

1 tablespoon red wine vinegar

½ teaspoon ground cumin

½ teaspoon sea salt

¼ teaspoon freshly ground black pepper

3 tablespoons olive oil

to serve

1 orange, segmented, peel and pith removed (optional)

1 tablespoon chopped celery leaves, or use flat-leaf (Italian) parsley

freshly ground black pepper

1. Preheat the oven to 180°C (350°F). Line 2 baking trays with baking paper.

2. In a large mixing bowl, toss the sweet potato, capsicum and onion with the oil, cumin and salt until well coated. Place the vegetables on a baking tray in a single layer and roast until tender and browned, about 40 minutes. Allow to cool.

3. On a separate baking tray, roast the walnuts until they are lightly golden and smell toasty, about 6 minutes.

4. Meanwhile, cook the rice according to the packet instructions or your preferred method. Drain and allow it to cool.

5. To make the dressing, whisk together the orange juice, orange zest, honey, vinegar, cumin, sea salt and pepper until well combined. Slowly dribble in the oil, whisking continuously, until well blended.

6. In a large mixing bowl, combine the cooked vegetables with the walnuts, rice, feta, cranberries, celery and chopped celery leaves. Pour in the dressing and toss to combine.

7. To serve, transfer the salad to a serving dish and garnish with orange segments, if using, celery leaves and pepper. Store in the refrigerator until ready to serve. This salad is best eaten on the day it is made.

summer potato salad

This salad loves summer. It loves casual dining, barbecues and paper plates. Serve it with grilled sausages, steak or barbecued ribs. Chicken is also good. Everyone will be back for a second helping. You can easily double the recipe.

Use new potatoes.

1 kg (2 lb 3 oz) new potatoes, scrubbed

½ teaspoon salt for the cooking water

250 g (9 oz/1 cup) mayonnaise

6 large eggs, hard-boiled

3 celery stalks, finely sliced

½ teaspoon sea salt

½ teaspoon freshly ground black pepper, plus extra to serve

to serve

2 tablespoons sliced fresh chives

1. Put the potatoes and salt in a medium saucepan and cover with cold water. Bring to the boil over medium–high heat and boil until tender, about 12–15 minutes, testing with the point of a sharp knife. Drain the potatoes, reserving 125 ml (4 fl oz/½ cup) of the cooking water, and return them to the saucepan over low heat for 1 minute to ensure any excess water has evaporated. Remove the potatoes from the saucepan and set aside to cool.

2. To make the dressing, whisk together the mayonnaise and 2 tablespoons of the cooking water until creamy. Add more cooking water until the desired consistency is achieved.

3. To make the salad, slice each potato into quarters and place in a large mixing bowl. Slice the eggs and add them to the mixing bowl along with the celery. Sprinkle with the sea salt and pepper. Pour in the dressing and toss to combine.

4. To serve, transfer the salad to a serving bowl and sprinkle with pepper and chives.

5. Store in the refrigerator until ready to serve. This salad is best eaten on the day it is made.

lemony potato salad

This salad is bound to be a new summer staple. The whisper of lemon and the freshness of dill and chives are lovely. Try it with fish or chicken.

Use kipfler (fingerling) potatoes or new potatoes.

1 kg (2 lb 3 oz) kipfler (fingerling) or new potatoes, scrubbed

½ teaspoon salt for the cooking water

250 g (9 oz/1 cup) crème fraîche or sour cream

2 tablespoons lemon juice

1 teaspoon lemon zest

1 tablespoon chopped fresh dill, plus extra to serve

1 tablespoon chopped fresh chives, plus extra to serve

½ teaspoon sea salt

½ teaspoon freshly ground black pepper, plus extra to serve

2 celery stalks, thinly sliced

6 small radishes, thinly sliced

1. Put the potatoes and salt in a medium saucepan and cover with cold water. Bring to the boil over medium–high heat and boil until tender, about 12–15 minutes, testing with the point of a sharp knife. Drain the potatoes, reserving 125 ml (4 fl oz/½ cup) of the cooking water, and return them to the saucepan over low heat for 1 minute to ensure any excess water has evaporated. Remove the potatoes from the saucepan and set aside to cool.

2. To make the dressing, whisk together the crème fraîche, lemon juice, lemon zest, dill, chives, sea salt and pepper until smooth. Add 2 tablespoons of the reserved cooking water and whisk until creamy, adding more cooking water until the desired consistency is achieved.

3. To make the salad, slice each potato into 1 cm (½ in) slices and place in a large mixing bowl. Add the celery and radishes. Pour in the dressing and toss to combine.

4. Transfer the salad to a serving bowl and sprinkle with dill, chives and pepper.

5. Store in the refrigerator until ready to serve. This salad is best eaten on the day it is made.

blue cheese potato salad

There's something about blue cheese that lifts a potato salad. Robust yet elegant, this salad pairs beautifully with beef.

Use waxy (boiling) potatoes; see pages 002–003 for a list of varieties.

1 kg (2 lb 3 oz) new potatoes, scrubbed

½ teaspoon salt for the cooking water

60 g (2 oz/½ cup) chopped pecans, or use walnuts

125 g (4½ oz/½ cup) mayonnaise

125 g (4½ oz/½ cup) Greek yoghurt

2 teaspoons balsamic vinegar

1 teaspoon honey, warmed

125 g (4½ oz/½ cup) blue cheese, crumbled

1 tablespoon chopped fresh chives, plus extra to serve

½ teaspoon freshly ground black pepper

3 celery stalks, sliced

1. Preheat the oven to 170°C (340°F) and line a baking tray with baking paper.

2. Put the potatoes and salt in a medium saucepan and cover with cold water. Bring to the boil over medium–high heat and boil until tender, about 12–15 minutes, testing with the point of a sharp knife. Drain the potatoes, reserving 125 ml (4 fl oz/½ cup) of the cooking water, and return them to the saucepan over low heat for 1 minute to ensure any excess water has evaporated. Remove the potatoes from the saucepan and set aside to cool.

3. Meanwhile, spread the pecans over the baking tray and roast until they are lightly golden and smell toasty, about 6 minutes.

4. To make the dressing, whisk together the mayonnaise, yoghurt, balsamic vinegar, honey and 2 tablespoons of the cooking water until creamy. Add more cooking water until the desired consistency is achieved. Stir in the blue cheese, chives and pepper. Taste the dressing and add sea salt if needed.

5. To make the salad, slice each potato into quarters. Place them in a large mixing bowl with the celery and pecans. Pour in the dressing and toss to combine.

6. Transfer the salad to a serving bowl and sprinkle with chives and pepper.

7. Store in the refrigerator until ready to serve. This salad is best eaten on the day it is made.

chocolate potato truffles

These little balls are smooth, chocolatey, rich and delicious – and, surprisingly, contain no cream or flour. If you'd rather not roll them in coconut, crushed walnuts also taste fantastic.

Use floury (starchy or roasting) potatoes; see pages 002–003 for a list of varieties.

3 small potatoes, about 300 g (10½ oz), peeled and cut into 2 cm (¾ in) pieces

¼ teaspoon salt for the cooking water

200 g (7 oz) dark chocolate (70% cocoa), chopped into small pieces

2 tablespoons coconut oil

2 tablespoons cold brewed coffee

2 tablespoons maple syrup

¼ teaspoon sea salt

45 g (1½ oz/½ cup) desiccated (shredded) coconut

1. Put the potatoes and salt in a small saucepan and cover with cold water. Bring to the boil over medium–high heat and boil until very tender, about 12 minutes, testing with the point of a sharp knife. Drain the potatoes and return to the saucepan over low heat for 1 minute to ensure any excess water has evaporated. Put through a ricer or mash well until very smooth.

2. Pour 2 cm (¾ in) of water into a small saucepan over medium–low heat. Put the chocolate and coconut oil in a heatproof bowl and sit the bowl on top of the saucepan, making sure it doesn't touch the water. Stir until the chocolate is smooth and glossy. Remove the bowl and place it on a tea towel (dish towel) on a work surface, taking care as the bowl may be hot. Mix in the coffee, maple syrup and sea salt until smooth.

3. Measure 230 g (8 oz/1 cup) of mashed potato into a medium mixing bowl. Pour half of the chocolate mixture over the mashed potato and stir well with a wooden spoon. Add the remaining chocolate mixture and beat until very smooth.

4. Place the desiccated coconut on a plate.

5. Roll tablespoons of the chocolate into balls between your hands and place them on the coconut. Roll the balls in the coconut until all sides are coated, then place on a clean plate and into the refrigerator to set.

6. Serve with coffee or tea after dinner for an elegant treat.

7. Store in an airtight container in the refrigerator for up to 3 days.

gingerbread sweet potato and brown bread ice cream

In this scrumptious ice cream – one of my favourites – the breadcrumbs are caramelised with brown sugar, cinnamon and ginger to provide a subtle contrast to the creamy sweet potato. It's a winning combination. I like to use dark rye bread, but any brown bread is delicious.

Use orange sweet potatoes.

for the ice cream

1 small–medium sweet potato, about 250 g (9 oz)

250 ml (8½ fl oz/1 cup) full-cream (whole) milk, chilled

80 g (2¾ oz/⅓ cup) caster (superfine) sugar

60 g (2 oz/⅓ cup) brown sugar

2 tablespoons maple syrup

2 tablespoons skim (no fat) milk powder

1 teaspoon ground cinnamon

½ teaspoon ground ginger

¼ teaspoon freshly grated nutmeg

¼ teaspoon sea salt

500 ml (17 fl oz/2 cups) thick (heavy) cream, chilled

for the brown breadcrumbs

100 g (3½ oz) brown bread, about 2 slices

80 g (2¾ oz/⅓ cup) caster (superfine) sugar

½ teaspoon ground cinnamon

¼ teaspoon ground ginger

¼ teaspoon sea salt

30 g (1 oz) unsalted butter, melted

1. Preheat the oven to 190°C (375°F) and line 2 baking trays with baking paper.

2. Scrub the sweet potato and pierce it a few times with a skewer. Wrap in foil, place on a baking tray and bake until tender, about 1 hour, checking with a skewer.

3. To make the brown breadcrumbs, process the bread, sugar, cinnamon, ginger and sea salt in a food processor until they resemble breadcrumbs. Tip the breadcrumbs into a bowl, pour the melted butter over them and stir until combined. Spread the breadcrumbs mixture over a baking tray and bake until deep brown, dry and caramelised, about 30 minutes. Remove the tray from the oven a few times to stir the breadcrumbs and ensure they brown evenly. Set aside to cool completely.

4. Meanwhile, in a large mixing bowl whisk the milk with the sugars, maple syrup, milk powder, cinnamon, ginger, nutmeg and sea salt until the sugars are dissolved, about 1 minute. Place in the refrigerator to chill while the sweet potato is cooking.

5. When cooked, allow the sweet potato to cool slightly, then peel and mash. Measure 180 g (6½ oz/¾ cup) of sweet potato and add it to a large mixing bowl.

6. Remove the milk mixture from the refrigerator and whisk again. Add the cream and whisk until combined, then stir this into the sweet potato. Blend until smooth using a hand-held blender.

7. Put the sweet potato mixture in the refrigerator until chilled. Churn in an ice cream maker or use an ice cream bowl attachment for a stand mixer as per the manufacturer's instructions.

8. Fold about half of the breadcrumbs through the ice cream. Spoon the ice cream into an airtight freezer-safe container and freeze for 3–4 hours.

9. To serve, scoop the ice cream into individual bowls and sprinkle with the remaining breadcrumbs.

10. Store in an airtight freezer-safe container in the freezer for up to 1 week. After this time it may start to become icy.

sweet potato and miso ice cream with spiced pepitas

Bored with the usual ice cream varieties? Once you taste the seductive, almost caramel notes of sweet potato and miso ice cream you'll be a convert. Stunning with a drizzle of honey and a sprinkling of spiced pepitas.

Use orange sweet potatoes.

for the ice cream

1 small–medium sweet potato, about 250 g (9 oz)

250 ml (8½ fl oz/1 cup) full-cream (whole) milk, chilled

115 g (4 oz/½ cup) caster (superfine) sugar

45 g (1½ oz/¼ cup) brown sugar

2 tablespoons white (shiro) miso paste

2 tablespoons skim (no fat) milk powder

1 teaspoon natural vanilla extract

¼ teaspoon sea salt

500 ml (17 fl oz/2 cups) thick (heavy) cream, chilled

for the spiced pepitas

75 g (2¾ oz/½ cup) pepitas (pumpkin seeds)

20 g (¾ oz) unsalted butter, melted

½ teaspoon grated orange zest

1 tablespoon brown sugar

½ teaspoon ground cinnamon

¼ teaspoon ground ginger

¼ teaspoon sea salt

to serve

honey to drizzle

1. Preheat the oven to 190°C (375°F) and line a baking tray with baking paper.

2. Scrub the sweet potato and pierce it a few times with a skewer. Wrap it in foil, place on a baking tray and bake until tender, about 1 hour, checking with a skewer.

3. Meanwhile, in a large mixing bowl whisk the milk with the sugars, miso paste, skim milk powder, vanilla extract and sea salt for about 1 minute. Place in the refrigerator to chill while the sweet potato is cooking.

4. Once cooked, allow the sweet potato to cool slightly, then peel and mash. Measure 180 g (6½ oz/¾ cup) of sweet potato and add it to a large mixing bowl.

5. Remove the milk mixture from the refrigerator and whisk again. Add the cream and whisk until combined, then stir this into the sweet potato. Blend until smooth using a hand-held blender.

6. Place the ice cream mixture back into the refrigerator until chilled. Churn in an ice cream maker or use an ice cream bowl attachment for a stand mixer as per the manufacturer's instructions.

7. Spoon the ice cream into an airtight freezer-safe container and freeze for 3–4 hours.

8. Preheat the oven to 180°C (350°F) and line a baking tray with baking paper.

9. To make the spiced pepitas, in a small mixing bowl stir together the pepitas, melted butter and orange zest until the seeds are coated in butter. In a separate bowl, combine the sugar, cinnamon, ginger and sea salt. Add the sugar mixture to the pepitas and stir until well combined. Spread in a single layer on the baking tray and bake until puffed and golden, about 20 minutes. Remove the tray from the oven a few times to stir the pepitas and ensure they cook evenly.

10. To serve, scoop the ice cream into individual bowls, drizzle with honey and sprinkle with spiced pepitas.

11. Store in an airtight freezer-safe container in the freezer for up to 1 week. After this time it may start to become icy.

sweet salty bark

This sweet salty bark is a real keeper. There's something about the combination of smooth milk chocolate and salty potato chips that is absolutely seductive. The first time you make it, you'll snap off a piece – just to try – and before you know it, you'll be reaching for another, and then just one more. It's that good.

Use plain salted crinkle-cut potato chips (crisps).

200 g (7 oz) milk chocolate, chopped into small pieces

2 teaspoons coconut oil

75 g (2¾ oz/1½ cups) roughly crushed crinkle-cut potato chips (crisps)

pinch of sea salt flakes (optional)

1. Line a 20 cm (8 in) baking pan with some baking paper.

2. Pour 2 cm (¾ in) of water into a small saucepan over medium–low heat. Put the chocolate and the coconut oil in a heatproof bowl and sit the bowl on top of the saucepan, making sure it doesn't touch the water. Stir until the chocolate is just melted and combined with the coconut oil. Remove the bowl and place it on a tea towel (dish towel) on a work surface, taking care as the bowl may be hot. Tip the crushed potato chips into the chocolate mixture and stir until all the chip pieces are coated.

3. Pour the mixture into the lined pan and use the back of a spoon to coax the mixture into the corners of the pan, tipping the pan if needed to ensure the chocolate is evenly distributed. Sprinkle with sea salt flakes, if desired. Place the pan in the refrigerator to set the chocolate.

4. Once the bark is completely set, snap it into rough pieces to serve.

5. Store in an airtight container in the refrigerator for up to 1 week.

dark chilli chocolate and potato chip bark

Perfect for after dinner or as a pick-me-up afternoon snack, this delicious treat has a seductive taste, with its combination of dark chocolate, chilli and salty potato chips.

Use plain salted crinkle-cut potato chips (crisps).

200 g (7 oz) dark chocolate (70% cocoa), chopped into small pieces

2 teaspoons coconut oil

½ teaspoon cayenne pepper, or to taste

75 g (2¾ oz/1½ cups) roughly crushed crinkle-cut potato chips (crisps)

pinch of sea salt flakes (optional)

1. Line a 20 cm (8 in) baking pan with some baking paper.

2. Pour 2 cm (¾ in) of water into a small saucepan over medium heat. Put the chocolate and coconut oil in a heatproof bowl and sit the bowl on the saucepan, making sure it doesn't touch the water. Stir until the chocolate is just melted and combined with the coconut oil. Remove the bowl and place it on a tea towel (dish towel) on a work surface, taking care as the bowl may be hot. Stir the cayenne pepper into the chocolate. Tip the crushed potato chips into the chocolate mixture and stir until all the chip pieces are coated.

3. Pour the mixture into the lined pan and use the back of a spoon to coax the mixture into the corners of the pan, tipping the pan if needed to ensure the chocolate is evenly distributed. Sprinkle with sea salt flakes, if desired. Place the pan in the refrigerator to set the chocolate.

4. Once the bark is completely set, snap it into rough pieces to serve.

5. Store in an airtight container in the refrigerator for up to 1 week.

knead & roll

wholemeal potato pie

Potatoes plus pie equals comfort food heaven. Make the pie crust wholemeal (whole-wheat) and add silverbeet (Swiss chard) to the filling and it's the centrepiece of a fine meal. Try it with a big green salad and some roasted carrots.

Use waxy potatoes; see pages 002–003 for a list of varieties.

for the filling

6 medium potatoes, about 1 kg (2 lb 3 oz), peeled and chopped into quarters

½ teaspoon salt for the cooking water

3 tablespoons olive oil

1 medium onion, diced

1 bunch silverbeet (Swiss chard) or 250 g (9 oz) baby English spinach leaves

½ teaspoon sea salt

½ teaspoon freshly ground black pepper

¼ teaspoon freshly grated nutmeg

185 g (6½ oz/1½ cups) grated cheddar cheese

for the pastry

450 g (1 lb/3 cups) wholemeal (whole-wheat) flour

250 g (9 oz) unsalted butter, cubed

1 teaspoon sea salt

80 ml (2½ fl oz/⅓ cup) cold water, as needed

1 egg, at room temperature

1. Put the potatoes and salt in a medium saucepan and cover with cold water. Bring to the boil and simmer until tender, about 15–20 minutes, testing with the point of a sharp knife. Drain the potatoes and return them to the saucepan over low heat for 1 minute to ensure any excess water has evaporated.

2. Meanwhile, heat 2 tablespoons of olive oil in a frying pan over medium heat and cook the onion until soft and golden, about 5 minutes.

3. To prepare the silverbeet, remove and discard the thick white stalks and slice the green leaves. Add to the frying pan and cook until wilted and softened, about 4 minutes. Remove from the heat and stir in the sea salt, pepper and nutmeg.

4. Transfer the potatoes to a large mixing bowl and very lightly mash them with a fork so that pieces of potato are still visible. Add the silverbeet mixture, cheese and 1 tablespoon of olive oil and mix together with a large metal spoon. Set aside until completely cold.

5. Preheat the oven to 200°C (400°F) and place a baking tray in the oven. You need a 23 cm (9 in) round pie dish (use a metal pie dish if you have one).

6. To make the pastry, process the flour, butter and sea salt in a food processor until it resembles fine breadcrumbs. Add the water, a little at a time, and process until it clumps together (you may not need all of the water). On a lightly floured work surface, knead the pastry until smooth, about 1 minute. Form the pastry into a disc with your hands and cover in plastic wrap. Refrigerate for 20 minutes.

7. Cut off a third of the pastry and set aside. On a lightly floured work surface, roll out the remaining two-thirds of the pastry until 3 mm (⅛ in) thick and large enough to line the pie dish. Carefully press the pastry into the pie dish, leaving a 5 mm (¼ in) overhang, and trim off the excess pastry. Combine the pastry trimmings with the remaining one-third of the pastry; this will be used for the pie top.

Recipe continues on next page.

wholemeal potato pie (continued)

8. Spoon the potato filling into the pastry shell and flatten with the back of the spoon. On a lightly floured work surface, roll the remaining pastry into a circle large enough to cover the pie, about 3 mm (⅛ in) thick. Wet your finger with water and dampen the edge of the pastry shell, then carefully lay the pastry top over the filling. Trim off the excess pastry, allowing a slight overhang. Use your fingers to pinch the edge of the pastry together for a decorative finish (or use a fork to press the edges together).

9. Cut a small hole in the centre of the pastry top, about 1 cm (½ in), to allow steam to escape. If desired, cut the pastry trimmings into decorative shapes and place them on the pastry top, using a small amount of water to make them stick.

10. Lightly beat the egg with 1 teaspoon of water to make a glaze. Generously brush the pastry top with the egg glaze.

11. Place the pie dish on the preheated baking tray and bake until the pastry is golden brown, about 40–45 minutes. Remove from the oven and place on a wire rack for 10 minutes before serving.

potato, caramelised onion and thyme focaccia

Sometimes I think I make this bread just because the house smells so heavenly as it bakes. It goes without saying that the bread tastes wonderful, too. Serve as a side for soup or slice through the middle to make fabulous sandwiches.

Use waxy potatoes; see pages 002–003 for a list of varieties.

2 medium potatoes, about 350 g (12½ oz), peeled and cut into 1 cm (½ in) cubes

¼ teaspoon salt for the cooking water

1 teaspoon honey

2¼ teaspoons dry yeast, about 7 g (¼ oz)

450 g (1 lb/3 cups) bread (strong) flour, or use plain (all-purpose) flour

150 g (5½ oz/1 cup) wholemeal (whole-wheat) flour

2 teaspoons fresh thyme leaves

2 teaspoons sea salt

½ teaspoon freshly ground black pepper

70 ml (2¼ fl oz) olive oil, plus extra to grease the bowl

15 g (½ oz) unsalted butter

1 medium onion, halved and sliced

2 teaspoons polenta

1 teaspoon sea salt flakes

1. Put the potatoes and salt in a small saucepan and cover with 500 ml (17 fl oz/2 cups) of cold water. Bring to the boil over medium–high heat and boil until very tender, about 8 minutes, testing with the point of a sharp knife. Drain the potatoes, reserving the cooking water, and return them to the saucepan over low heat for 1 minute to ensure any excess water has evaporated. Set aside to cool.

2. Measure 400 ml (13½ fl oz) of the potato cooking water into a small measuring jug, stir in the honey and cool to lukewarm, about 40–42°C (104–107°F). Sprinkle the yeast over the cooking water and stir gently. Set aside until the top of the water is foamy, about 5–10 minutes.

3. Combine the flours, thyme, sea salt and pepper in a large mixing bowl or the bowl of a stand mixer. Stir in the yeast and water mixture and 2 tablespoons of olive oil.

4. If using a stand mixer, insert the dough hook and knead the dough until smooth and elastic, about 10 minutes. Or, turn the dough onto a lightly floured work surface and knead until smooth and elastic, about 10 minutes. Shape the dough into a ball. Grease a large mixing bowl with olive oil. Place the dough in the bowl and cover with plastic wrap. Set aside in a warm place until doubled in size, about 1 hour.

5. While the dough is rising, caramelise the onion. Heat 2 teaspoons of olive oil and the butter in a small frying pan over medium heat and cook the onion, stirring occasionally, until there are touches of gold on the onion, about 4 minutes. Reduce the heat to medium–low and cook, stirring occasionally, until the onion is very soft and golden, about 20 minutes. Set aside to cool.

6. Turn the dough onto a lightly floured work surface and knead in the potatoes and onion until evenly distributed. Return the dough to the bowl, cover with plastic wrap and set aside in a warm place for a further 30 minutes.

7. Preheat the oven to 220°C (430°F). Sprinkle a baking tray with 2 teaspoons of polenta.

8. Turn the dough onto a lightly floured work surface. Using your hands, pat it into a rectangle about 30 x 25 cm (12 x 10 in) and transfer to the baking tray. Brush with 1 tablespoon of olive oil. Cover loosely with plastic wrap and set aside in a warm place to rise again, about 30 minutes. Remove the plastic wrap and use your fingers to create dimples in the top of the dough. Sprinkle with sea salt flakes.

9. Bake until golden brown, about 20–25 minutes. When cooked, the loaf will sound hollow when tapped. Transfer to a wire rack to cool.

potato, brie and caramelised onion tart

I make this tart when I want something with a bit of wow factor that's not too difficult. The caramelised onions make it particularly gorgeous. This tart is lovely accompanied by a leafy salad with a vinegary dressing.

Use new potatoes.

for the pastry

225 g (8 oz/1½ cups) plain (all-purpose) flour

100 g (3½ oz) unsalted butter, cold, diced

½ teaspoon sea salt

2 tablespoons cold water

for the filling

1 tablespoon olive oil

30 g (1 oz) unsalted butter

2 medium red onions, halved and sliced

2 medium potatoes, about 350 g (12½ oz), sliced
  into 5 mm (¼ in) slices

¼ teaspoon salt for the cooking water

25 g (1 oz/¼ cup) grated parmesan cheese

170 ml (5½ fl oz/⅔ cup) thick (heavy) cream

3 large eggs, at room temperature

¼ teaspoon sea salt

¼ teaspoon freshly ground black pepper

100 g (3½ oz) brie, cut into 5 mm (¼ in) slices

1 teaspoon fresh thyme leaves, plus extra
  to serve

1. Preheat the oven to 200°C (400°F) and place a baking tray in the oven. You need a 23 cm (9 in) round flan (tart) pan with fluted sides and removable base.

2. To make the pastry, combine the flour, butter and sea salt in a food processor and pulse until the texture of fine breadcrumbs. Add the water and pulse until the dough starts to clump together. On a lightly floured work surface, knead the pastry until smooth, about 1 minute. Form the pastry into a disc with your hands and cover in plastic wrap. Refrigerate for 20 minutes.

3. To make the filling, heat the olive oil and butter in a medium frying pan over medium heat. Add the sliced onions and fry, stirring occasionally, until you start to see touches of gold on the onions, about 4 minutes. Reduce the heat to medium–low and cook, stirring occasionally, until the onions are very soft and golden brown, about 20 minutes.

4. Put the potatoes and salt in a small saucepan and cover with cold water. Bring to the boil over medium–high heat and boil until tender, about 6–8 minutes, testing with the point of a sharp knife. Drain the potatoes and return them to the saucepan over low heat for 1 minute to ensure any excess water has evaporated.

5. Meanwhile, on a lightly floured work surface, roll out the pastry into a circle about 3 mm (⅛ in) thick. Line the flan pan with the pastry, taking care when pressing into the fluted sides. Trim the overhang, leaving a 5 mm (¼ in) lip around the edge of the pan to allow for shrinkage. Place the pan on the baking tray. Prick the pastry with a fork in a few places and chill in the refrigerator for 15 minutes.

6. To blind bake the pastry, cover it with a sheet of baking paper and fill with pie weights or uncooked rice. Bake for 15 minutes. Remove the weights and the baking paper and return the pastry to the oven until the pastry looks dry and lightly golden, about 10 minutes. Sprinkle the pastry with the parmesan cheese and set aside for 5 minutes.

7. Reduce the oven heat to 170°C (340°F).

8. In a medium mixing bowl, whisk the cream, eggs, sea salt and pepper together until smooth.

9. To assemble the tart for baking, spread the onions over the parmesan in the pastry case. Layer the potato slices on top of the onions, followed by the brie. Sprinkle with the thyme leaves. Gently pour the egg mixture over the top.

10. Bake the tart until it is puffed and golden, about 40–45 minutes. Sprinkle with thyme and allow to cool for a few minutes before removing from the pan and slicing.

seedy potato crackers

These crackers are as wholesome as they are versatile. Have them with a sliver of your favourite cheese, crumble them over a salad for added crunch, or just enjoy on their own.

Use floury (starchy or roasting) potatoes; see pages 002–003 for a list of varieties.

3 medium–large potatoes, about 600 g (1 lb 5 oz), peeled and cut into 2 cm (¾ in) cubes

¼ teaspoon salt for the cooking water

1 teaspoon sea salt

40 g (1½ oz/¼ cup) sesame seeds

45 g (1½ oz/¼ cup) black chia seeds

45 g (1½ oz/¼ cup) linseeds (flax seeds)

25 g (1 oz/¼ cup) grated parmesan cheese

40 g (1½ oz/¼ cup) potato starch

1 egg yolk

2 teaspoons olive oil

1. Put the potatoes and salt in a small saucepan and cover with cold water. Bring to the boil over medium–high heat and boil until very tender, about 12 minutes, testing with the point of a sharp knife. Drain the potatoes and return them to the saucepan over low heat for 1 minute to ensure any excess water has evaporated. Put the potato through a ricer or mash until very smooth.

2. Measure 460 g (1 lb/2 cups) of mashed potato into a large mixing bowl or the bowl of a stand mixer. Add the sea salt, sesame seeds, chia seeds, linseeds, parmesan, potato starch, egg yolk and olive oil and mix until thoroughly combined, about 1 minute.

3. Form the dough into a ball, put in a medium bowl and cover with plastic wrap. Refrigerate for at least 1 hour or overnight.

4. Preheat the oven to 160°C (320°F) and line 2 baking trays with baking paper.

5. Divide the dough into 4 equal portions. Take 1 portion and flatten it between 2 sheets of baking paper with your hands. Still between the baking paper, roll the pastry into a rectangle about 2–3 mm (1/16–1/8 in) thick, making sure it will fit on your tray. Peel off the top sheet of baking paper and mark the dough into rectangles, about 5 x 2.5 cm (2 x 1 in), slicing all the way through the dough. Pick up the dough, leaving it on the baking paper, and place on a baking tray. Repeat with another portion of dough, placing it on the second baking tray. Cook the dough in 2 batches, so while the first 2 sheets are cooking you can roll and prepare the next 2 sheets of dough.

6. Bake for 40–45 minutes or until crisp and browned. Swap and turn the trays every 15 minutes. (If necessary, snap off the outside pieces if they're cooked before the middle pieces and place them on a wire rack.) Cool on the trays for 10 minutes before transferring to a wire rack until completely cold.

7. Store in an airtight container for up to 5 days.

quick cheesy potato bread

This is perfect with soup on a chilly winter's evening. Pop it in the oven while the soup is simmering, and make sure you eat it warm! It even stands up to crumbling or dunking into the soup. Try a piece with a smear of butter and a drizzle of honey – perfect!

Use floury (starchy or roasting) potatoes; see pages 002–003 for a list of varieties.

225 g (8 oz/1½ cups) plain (all-purpose) flour, plus extra for dusting

2 medium potatoes, about 350 g (12½ oz), peeled and cut into 2 cm (¾ in) cubes

¼ teaspoon salt for the cooking water

2 large eggs, at room temperature

2 teaspoons baking powder

1 teaspoon sea salt

1 tablespoon olive oil

75 g (2¾ oz/¾ cup) finely grated parmesan cheese

1 teaspoon melted butter or milk

1. Preheat the oven to 200°C (400°F). Line a baking tray with baking paper and sprinkle with a little plain flour.

2. Put the potatoes and salt in a small saucepan and cover with cold water. Bring to the boil over medium–high heat and boil until very tender, about 12 minutes, testing with the point of a sharp knife. Drain the potatoes and return to the saucepan over low heat for 1 minute to ensure any excess water has evaporated. Put the potato through a ricer or mash until smooth.

3. In a small mixing bowl, whisk the eggs together.

4. In a medium mixing bowl, whisk the flour, baking powder and sea salt until combined.

5. Measure 230 g (8 oz/1 cup) of mashed potato into a large mixing bowl. Pour in the olive oil and beat until creamy. Add the eggs and mix until completely incorporated. Stir through the parmesan. Add the flour mixture and stir until just combined.

6. On a lightly floured work surface, knead the dough gently until it just comes together. Shape into a round loaf and score the top into 8 wedges with a sharp knife. Brush the top of the loaf with 1 teaspoon melted butter or milk.

7. Bake until golden, about 30 minutes. When cooked, the loaf will sound hollow when tapped.

buttermilk potato bread

This bread is light and soft, with just a hint of potato. It's delicious fresh out of the oven with butter, on sandwiches, toasted – it's an all-round winner!

Use floury (starchy or roasting) potatoes; see pages 002–003 for a list of varieties.

2 medium potatoes, about 350 g (12½ oz), peeled and cut into 2 cm (¾ in) pieces

½ teaspoon salt for the cooking water

375 ml (12½ fl oz/1½ cups) buttermilk

1 teaspoon honey

2¼ teaspoons dry yeast, about 7 g (¼ oz)

450 g (1 lb/3 cups) plain (all-purpose) flour, plus extra for dusting

300 g (10½ oz/2 cups) bread (strong) flour, or use plain (all-purpose) flour

2 teaspoons sea salt

80 ml (2½ fl oz/⅓ cup) olive oil, plus extra to grease the bowl

15 g (½ oz) unsalted butter, melted, plus extra to grease the loaf pan

1. Put the potatoes and salt in a small saucepan and cover with cold water. Bring to the boil over medium–high heat and boil until very tender, about 12 minutes, testing with the point of a sharp knife. Drain the potatoes and return them to the saucepan over low heat for 1 minute to ensure any excess water has evaporated. Put the potato through a ricer or mash thoroughly until smooth.

2. In a medium saucepan over low heat or in short bursts in the microwave, warm the buttermilk to lukewarm, about 40–42°C (104–107°F). This won't take long. Stir in the honey. Sprinkle the yeast over the buttermilk and stir gently. Set aside until the top of the milk is foamy, about 5–10 minutes.

3. In a large mixing bowl or the bowl of a stand mixer, combine the flours and the sea salt.

4. Measure 230 g (8 oz/1 cup) of mashed potato into a mixing bowl or the bowl of a stand mixer, add the olive oil and stir until smooth. Add about half of the buttermilk to the potato and stir until smooth. Repeat with the remaining buttermilk. Add the flour mixture and stir until roughly combined.

5. If using a stand mixer, insert the dough hook and knead the dough until smooth and elastic, about 10 minutes. Or, turn the dough onto a lightly floured work surface and knead until smooth and elastic, about 10 minutes. Shape the dough into a ball.

6. Grease a large mixing bowl with olive oil. Place the ball of dough in the bowl and cover with plastic wrap. Set aside in a warm place until doubled in size, about 1 hour.

7. Preheat the oven to 190°C (375°F). Grease a 23 x 13 x 7 cm (9 x 5 x 3 in) loaf (bar) pan with butter.

8. Turn the dough onto a lightly floured work surface. It will deflate as you remove it from the bowl. Pat it out into a rectangle with the short side the same size as the long side of your loaf pan. Roll tightly from the short side and place into the prepared loaf pan, seam side down. Cover with plastic wrap and set aside in a warm place until doubled in size, about 30 minutes. Remove the plastic wrap and brush the dough with melted butter.

9. Bake until golden brown, about 35 minutes. When cooked, the loaf will sound hollow when tapped and the internal temperature of the loaf will be 90–95°C (195–205°F). Leave in the pan for 5 minutes, then remove and place on a wire rack to cool before cutting.

potato and chorizo loaf

This is a versatile loaf that is equally good hot or cold. Served straight out of the oven with a salad of cherry tomatoes and mixed greens, it's the perfect light summer lunch. Allow the loaf to cool and you've got picnic fare. Leftovers are lunchbox favourites. Excellent as the base for savoury new French toast (page 100), this loaf is delicious however you serve it.

Use waxy potatoes; see pages 002–003 for a list of varieties.

2 small–medium potatoes, about 280 g (10 oz), peeled and cut into 1 cm (½ in) cubes

½ teaspoon salt for the cooking water

125 g (4½ oz) chorizo

2 teaspoons olive oil

1 small red onion, diced

1 small red capsicum (bell pepper), seeded and diced

40 g (1½ oz) baby English spinach leaves, sliced

375 g (13 oz/2½ cups) plain (all-purpose) flour

185 g (6½ oz/1½ cups) grated cheddar cheese

125 g (4½ oz) unsalted butter, cold, diced

1 teaspoon sea salt

2 teaspoons baking powder

250 ml (8½ fl oz/1 cup) full-cream (whole) milk

2 large eggs, at room temperature

1. Preheat the oven to 180°C (350°F) and line a baking tray with baking paper.

2. Put the potatoes and salt in a small saucepan and cover with cold water. Bring to the boil over medium–high heat and boil until very tender, about 8 minutes, testing with the point of a sharp knife. Drain the potatoes and return them to the saucepan over low heat for a minute to ensure any excess water has evaporated. Set aside to cool.

3. Quarter the chorizo lengthways and chop each long quarter into slices, about 5 mm (⅛ in). Heat the olive oil in a medium frying pan over medium heat and cook the chorizo, onion and red capsicum until the chorizo is sizzling and golden brown and the onion and capsicum are tender, stirring occasionally, about 10 minutes. Add the baby spinach to the pan and stir until the spinach is wilted, about 1 minute. Remove the pan from the heat and stir in the cubes of cooked potato. Set aside to cool while you make the dough.

4. In a food processor, pulse the flour, 125 g (4½ oz/ 1 cup) of the cheese, the butter, sea salt and baking powder until it resembles breadcrumbs. Add the milk and 1 egg and pulse until the dough starts to clump together. Form the dough into a flat disc, cover in plastic wrap and refrigerate for 20 minutes.

5. On a lightly floured work surface, knead the dough until smooth, about 1 minute. Flour your rolling pin and roll the dough out to a 30 x 20 cm (12 x 8 in) rectangle. With the long side of the dough facing you, spread the potato and chorizo filling over the dough, leaving a 2 cm (¾ in) border on the long edge furthest away from you. Sprinkle the filling with the remaining cheddar cheese. Roll up from the long side, enclosing the filling.

6. Place on the baking tray, with the seam of the log underneath. Whisk 1 egg and 1 teaspoon of water together and brush over the dough.

7. Bake until golden, about 30 minutes. Set aside for 5 minutes before slicing.

sweet potato sticky buns

With a layer of caramel and pecans, a cinnamon swirl and a hint of orange in the sweet potato dough, these sticky buns will make you want to lick the plate.

Use orange sweet potato.

for the dough

1 small sweet potato, about 180 g (6½ oz), peeled and cut into 2.5 cm (1 in) pieces

125 ml (4 fl oz/½ cup) full-cream (whole) milk

55 g (2 oz/¼ cup) caster (superfine) sugar, plus 1 teaspoon extra

2¼ teaspoons dry yeast, about 7 g (¼ oz)

450 g (1 lb/3 cups) plain (all-purpose) flour

¼ teaspoon sea salt

3 eggs, at room temperature

125 g (4½ oz) unsalted butter, melted, plus extra to grease the bowl

½ teaspoon grated orange zest

1 teaspoon cold water

for the caramel

125 g (4½ oz/1 cup) chopped pecans

165 g (6 oz) unsalted butter, plus extra to grease the pan

125 g (4½ oz/⅔ cup) dark brown sugar

170 ml (5½ fl oz/⅔ cup) thick (heavy) cream

80 ml (2½ fl oz/⅓ cup) maple syrup

½ teaspoon sea salt

for the filling

90 g (3 oz/¾ cup) chopped pecans

125 g (4½ oz) unsalted butter, softened

95 g (3¼ oz/½ cup) dark brown sugar

1 teaspoon ground cinnamon

¼ teaspoon freshly grated nutmeg

¼ teaspoon sea salt

1. Preheat the oven to 170°C (340°F) and line a baking tray with baking paper.

2. Spread 215 g (7½ oz/1¾ cups) of pecans (i.e. all the pecans, including for the caramel and the filling) on the tray and roast in the oven until they are lightly golden and smell toasty, about 6 minutes. Set aside.

3. For the dough put the sweet potato in a small saucepan and cover with cold water. Bring to the boil over medium–high heat and boil until very tender, about 12 minutes, testing with the point of a sharp knife. Drain the sweet potato and return them to the saucepan over low heat for 1 minute to ensure any excess water has evaporated. Put the sweet potato through a ricer or mash thoroughly until very smooth.

4. In a medium saucepan over low heat or in short bursts in the microwave, warm the milk to lukewarm, about 40–42°C (104–107°F). This won't take long. Stir in 1 teaspoon of caster sugar. Sprinkle the yeast over the milk and stir gently. Set aside until the top of the milk is foamy, about 5–10 minutes.

5. In a large mixing bowl, combine the flour, 55 g (2 oz/¼ cup) of caster sugar and the sea salt.

Recipe continues on next page.

sweet potato
sticky buns (continued)

6. In a small mixing bowl, whisk 2 eggs together.

7. Measure 125 g (4½ oz/½ cup) of sweet potato into a large mixing bowl or the bowl of a stand mixer. Add the melted butter and orange zest and stir until very smooth. Add half of the milk and yeast mixture and stir until smooth. Repeat with the remaining milk and yeast mixture. Add the 2 whisked eggs and stir until completely incorporated. Add the flour mixture and stir until roughly combined.

8. If using a stand mixer, insert the dough hook and knead the dough until smooth and elastic, about 10 minutes. Or, turn the dough onto a lightly floured work surface and knead until smooth and elastic, about 10 minutes. Shape the dough into a ball.

9. Grease a large mixing bowl with butter. Place the ball of dough in the bowl and cover with plastic wrap. Set aside in a warm place until doubled in size, about 1¼–1½ hours.

10. To make the caramel, melt the butter in a medium saucepan over medium heat. Add the dark brown sugar, cream, maple syrup and sea salt, and stir until the caramel starts to boil. At this stage the caramel will froth and start to rise in the saucepan. Turn the heat down to medium–low and simmer until dark and glossy, stirring occasionally, about 5 minutes.

11. Grease a 33 x 22 x 5 cm (13 x 8¾ x 2 in) baking pan with butter. Pour 1½ cups of the caramel into the baking pan and swirl to coat the bottom and sides. Sprinkle 90 g (3 oz/ ¾ cup) of the pecans over the caramel. Set aside the rest of the caramel and 35 g (1¼ oz/ ¼ cup) of pecans.

12. To make the filling, in a large mixing bowl or the bowl of a stand mixer, beat together the softened butter, dark brown sugar, cinnamon, nutmeg and sea salt until light and fluffy, about 2 minutes.

13. Tip the dough onto a lightly floured work surface. It will deflate as you remove it from the bowl. Knead for 1 minute until smooth, then shape the dough into a rough rectangle with your hands. Using a lightly floured rolling pin, roll the dough into a 40 x 30 cm (1 ft 3¾ x 12 in) rectangle with the long side facing you.

14. Spread the dough with the filling, leaving a 2.5 cm (1 in) strip along the edge furthest away from you. Sprinkle with 90 g (3 oz/¾ cup) of pecans. Roll up from the long side closest to you, patting the ends in if necessary. Tuck the seam side of the log underneath and slice into 12 equal slices. Tip each piece, cut side up, onto a work surface and pat back into a circle with your hands. Place the rolls on top of the caramel and pecans in the baking pan, evenly spaced with 3 rolls along the short side of the baking pan and 4 rolls along the long side of the baking pan. Cover with plastic wrap and put in a warm place until doubled in size, about 50–60 minutes.

15. Preheat the oven to 180°C (350°F).

16. Whisk 1 egg and 1 teaspoon of cold water together and brush over the rolls. Bake until the rolls are golden brown and the caramel is bubbling, about 45 minutes. Cover loosely with foil if the rolls are browning too quickly. Place the baking pan on a wire rack to cool. After 5 minutes, spoon over the reserved caramel and sprinkle with the reserved pecans.

17. Serve warm or at room temperature.

pork, potato and green apple pie

The filling of this pie has a touch of sweetness that's the perfect balance for the savoury cheddar pastry. Serve with steamed vegetables or a lightly dressed green salad.

Use waxy potatoes; see pages 002–003 for a list of varieties.

for the filling

700 g (1 lb 9 oz) pork shoulder, trimmed and cut into 3 cm (1¼ in) pieces

1½ tablespoons plain (all-purpose) flour

2–3 tablespoons vegetable oil

1 large onion, diced

1 celery stalk, sliced

1 large carrot, halved lengthways and thinly sliced

250 ml (8½ fl oz/1 cup) apple cider

250 ml (8½ fl oz/1 cup) chicken stock (low-salt)

3 small potatoes, about 350 g (12½ oz), peeled and cut into 2 cm (¾ in) cubes

2 large granny smith apples or other tart cooking apples, peeled, cored and sliced

1 bay leaf

2 teaspoons fresh thyme leaves

½ teaspoon sea salt

¼ teaspoon freshly ground black pepper

for the pastry

185 g (6½ oz/1¼ cups) plain (all-purpose) flour

125 g (4½ oz) unsalted butter, cold, cut into cubes

60 g (2 oz/½ cup) grated cheddar cheese

½ teaspoon sea salt

60 ml (2 fl oz/¼ cup) cold water

1 egg, at room temperature

1. Put the pork pieces and the flour in a large plastic bag. Twist the top closed and shake to cover the pork pieces in flour.

2. Heat 1 tablespoon of vegetable oil in a large frying pan over medium–high heat and add half of the pork pieces, turning them until all sides are browned. Remove the pork pieces from the frying pan and set aside on a large plate. Add up to 1 tablespoon more vegetable oil to the frying pan if needed and brown the remaining pork. Set aside on the plate with the rest of the browned pork.

3. Reduce the heat to medium and add up to 1 tablespoon more vegetable oil to the frying pan if needed. Cook the onion, celery and carrot until softened, about 5 minutes, stirring occasionally. Pour in the apple cider and chicken stock and bring to the boil. Add the browned pork, potatoes, apples, bay leaf, thyme, sea salt and pepper and bring back to the boil. Reduce the heat to low and simmer, covered, stirring occasionally, until the pork, potatoes and apples are tender and the sauce has thickened, about 60 minutes.

4. Remove the bay leaf and taste the filling, adding more sea salt and pepper if needed. Transfer the filling to a 23 cm (9 in) pie dish and allow to cool slightly.

5. Preheat the oven to 200°C (400°F) and place a baking tray in the oven.

6. To make the pastry top, process the flour, butter, cheese and sea salt in a food processor until it resembles fine breadcrumbs. Add the water and process until it clumps together. On a lightly floured work surface, knead the pastry until smooth, about 1 minute. Form the pastry into a disc with your hands and cover in plastic wrap. Refrigerate for 20 minutes.

7. On a lightly floured work surface, roll out the pastry until it is 3 mm (⅛ in) thick. Cut 2 narrow strips from the pastry, about 2 cm (¾ in) wide, ensuring the remaining pastry is large enough to cover the pie dish. Wet your finger with cold water and run it around the rim of the pie dish to dampen it so the pastry will stick, then press the narrow pastry strips onto the rim of the dish. Wet your finger with water and dampen the top of the pastry strips, then carefully lay the pastry over the filling and pat down onto the pastry strips. Trim off the excess pastry, allowing a slight overhang. Pinch the edges of the pastry for a decorative finish.

8. Cut a small hole in the centre of the pastry, about 1 cm (½ in), to allow steam to escape.

9. Lightly beat the egg with 1 teaspoon of water and generously brush the pastry with the egg glaze. Place the pie dish on the preheated baking tray and bake until the pastry is golden brown and the filling is bubbling, about 45 minutes. Remove from the oven and place on a wire rack for 10 minutes before serving.

sweeten

luscious chocolate potato cake

This beautiful moist cake is, without question, my preferred chocolate cake. Made in a bundt pan, it's a real showstopper! Serve the cake with whipped cream or vanilla ice cream, or both.

Use floury (starchy or roasting) potatoes; see pages 002–003 for a list of varieties.

for the cake

250 g (9 oz) unsalted butter, at room temperature, cubed, plus extra to grease the pan

85 g (3 oz/⅔ cup) unsweetened (Dutch) cocoa powder, sifted, plus extra to dust the pan

3 small potatoes, about 300 g (10½ oz), peeled and cut into 2 cm (¾ in) pieces

375 g (13 oz/2½ cups) plain (all-purpose) flour, sifted

2 teaspoons instant coffee powder, sifted

2 teaspoons baking powder

1 teaspoon sea salt

4 large eggs, at room temperature

250 ml (8½ fl oz/1 cup) buttermilk, at room temperature

170 g (6 oz/¾ cup) caster (superfine) sugar

140 g (5 oz/¾ cup) brown sugar

2 teaspoons natural vanilla extract

for the ganache

190 ml (6½ fl oz/¾ cup) thick (heavy) cream

200 g (7 oz) dark chocolate (70%)

¼ teaspoon sea salt flakes (optional)

1. Preheat the oven to 180°C (350°F). Grease a 24 cm (9½ in) bundt pan with butter and dust with 2 teaspoons of sifted cocoa powder, shaking out any excess.

2. Put the potatoes in a small saucepan and cover with cold water. Bring to the boil over medium–high heat and boil until very tender, about 12 minutes, testing with the point of a sharp knife. Drain the potatoes and return them to the saucepan over low heat for 1 minute to ensure any excess water has evaporated. Pass through a ricer or mash until very smooth. Set aside to cool to room temperature.

3. In a large mixing bowl, whisk together the flour, cocoa powder, coffee powder, baking powder and sea salt. Set aside.

4. In a medium mixing bowl, whisk the eggs until well combined. Set aside.

5. Measure 230 g (8 oz/1 cup) of mashed potato into a separate large mixing bowl. Using a wooden spoon, stir 60 ml (2 fl oz/¼ cup) of the buttermilk into the potato and beat until smooth. Add the remaining buttermilk to the potato and stir until smooth.

6. In a separate large mixing bowl or the bowl of a stand mixer, beat the butter and sugars until light and fluffy, about 4 minutes. Add the whisked eggs, about a quarter at a time, mixing until each addition is completely incorporated before adding the next. Stir the vanilla extract into the cake batter.

7. Stir about one-third of the flour mixture into the cake batter until just incorporated. Next, stir in half of the potato/buttermilk mixture. Repeat with a further third of the flour mixture followed by the rest of the potato/buttermilk mixture. Lastly, fold the remaining flour into the batter.

8. Pour the cake batter evenly into the prepared pan and lightly smooth the top with a spatula. Place the bundt pan on a baking tray and bake until a toothpick or skewer inserted into the cake comes out clean, about 50 minutes. If you press the cake lightly with your finger it should bounce back. Don't worry if there are cracks in the top of the cake as they will be underneath when the cake is served.

9. Cool the cake in the pan for 10 minutes before turning out onto a wire rack.

10. When the cake is cool, make the ganache. Heat the cream in a small saucepan over medium heat until steaming and almost boiling. While the cream is heating, chop the chocolate into small pieces and put in a medium mixing bowl. Pour the hot cream over the chocolate and let it sit undisturbed for 1 minute, then stir continuously until the chocolate is melted and the ganache is smooth and glossy. Slowly pour the ganache over the cake and sprinkle with sea salt flakes, if desired.

11. Transfer the cake to a serving plate, to be the star of the table. Store left-over cake in the refrigerator in an airtight container for up to 3 days.

gingerbread sweet potato cheesecake

You may be surprised that a cheesecake this good contains a vegetable, but it's bound to induce a contented smile – maybe even a little murmur of satisfaction. Creamy and delicious, it also looks spectacular when you bring it to the table. Serve the cheesecake with whipped cream or vanilla ice cream – or both!

Use orange sweet potatoes.

for the base

150 g (5½ oz) digestive biscuits (or use graham crackers), crushed

60 g (2 oz/½ cup) chopped pecans

1 teaspoon ground ginger

75 g (2¾ oz) unsalted butter, melted

for the filling

1 medium–large sweet potato, about 500 g (1 lb 2 oz)

60 ml (2 fl oz/¼ cup) maple syrup

750 g (1 lb 11 oz) cream cheese (full-fat), at room temperature

55 g (2 oz/¼ cup) caster (superfine) sugar

95 g (3¼ oz/½ cup) brown sugar

1 teaspoon ground cinnamon

½ teaspoon ground ginger

¼ teaspoon freshly grated nutmeg

¼ teaspoon sea salt

3 large eggs, at room temperature

for the topping

60 g (2 oz) unsalted butter

45 g (1½ oz/¼ cup) brown sugar

60 ml (2 fl oz/¼ cup) maple syrup

60 ml (2 fl oz/¼ cup) thick (heavy) cream

¼ teaspoon sea salt

1. Preheat the oven to 190°C (375°F) and line a baking tray with baking paper. Line the base of a 23 cm (9 in) springform pan with baking paper.

2. Scrub the sweet potato and pierce it a few times with a skewer. Wrap in foil, place on the baking tray and bake until completely tender, about 1–1¼ hours, checking with a skewer.

3. Meanwhile, for the base, process the biscuits and pecans in a food processor until they are the texture of fine breadcrumbs. Add the ground ginger and process for a few seconds. Add the butter and process until the crumbs start to clump together. Press into the bottom and part way up the sides of the springform pan. Bake for 10 minutes. Set aside to cool.

4. Once the sweet potato is cooked, reduce the oven temperature to 180°C (350°F).

5. Allow the cooked sweet potato to cool slightly, then peel and mash. Measure 375 g (13 oz/ 1½ cups) of sweet potato into the cleaned bowl of the food processor along with the maple syrup and process until a smooth purée. Transfer to another bowl and set aside to cool.

6. Process the cream cheese in the cleaned food processor until smooth. Add the sugars, cinnamon, ginger, nutmeg and sea salt and process until smooth, stopping to scrape down the side of the bowl with a spatula as needed. Add the sweet potato mixture and process until blended. Add the eggs, one at a time, processing until each is incorporated before adding the

next. Stop the food processor and scrape down the side of the bowl with a spatula, then process until creamy. Pour the cheesecake filling over the biscuit base and smooth the top with a spatula.

7. Place on a baking tray and bake until the cheesecake is just set with a slight wobble in the middle, about 50–55 minutes. Turn off the oven. Leave the cheesecake in the oven with the door slightly ajar for 1 hour. Remove the cheesecake from the oven and run the tip of a sharp knife between the cheesecake and the inside of the pan. Place the cheesecake, still in the pan, on a wire rack until cool.

8. Meanwhile, make the topping. In a small saucepan over medium heat, melt the butter and stir in the sugar and maple syrup until the sugar is dissolved and the mixture is smooth. Bring to the boil and simmer for 3 minutes, reducing the heat to medium–low if the caramel is bubbling up the saucepan. Pour in the cream and stir until smooth. Bring back to the boil over medium heat and simmer for a further 1 minute. Remove from the heat and stir in the sea salt. Set aside to cool.

9. With the cheesecake still in the pan, pour the cool caramel over the top of the cheesecake and spread to the edges. Cover and refrigerate for at least 3 hours before serving, or overnight.

10. To serve, remove the cheesecake from the pan and transfer to a serving plate.

11. Store left-over cheesecake in the refrigerator in an airtight container for up to 3 days.

potato and earl grey tea cake

The potatoes in this tea cake give it a beautiful moist texture, while the sultanas soaked in earl grey tea add a wonderful flavour. It's the perfect remedy for that afternoon energy slump. Slice and serve with butter and a cup of tea or glass of milk.

Use floury (starchy or roasting) potatoes; see pages 002–003 for a list of varieties.

250 ml (8½ fl oz/1 cup) full-cream (whole) milk

2 earl grey tea bags (or use 2 teaspoons earl grey tea leaves)

125 g (4½ oz/1 cup) sultanas (golden raisins)

2 teaspoons grated lemon zest

3 small potatoes, about 300 g (10½ oz), peeled and cut into 2 cm (¾ in) pieces

225 g (8 oz/1½ cups) plain (all-purpose) flour

1½ teaspoons baking powder

1 tablespoon maple syrup

1 large egg, at room temperature, whisked

125 g (4½ oz/1 cup) chopped walnuts

140 g (5 oz/¾ cup) brown sugar

1. Heat the milk until just boiling. Place the teabags in a small measuring jug and pour the milk over them. Infuse for 5 minutes and then discard the tea bags.

2. In a small mixing bowl, pour the milk over the sultanas and lemon zest, stirring to combine. Set aside for 2 hours or overnight in the refrigerator to allow the sultanas to plump up and absorb the infused milk.

3. Put the potatoes in a small saucepan and cover with cold water. Bring to the boil over medium–high heat and boil until very tender, about 12 minutes, testing with the point of a sharp knife. Drain the potatoes and return them to the saucepan over low heat for 1 minute to ensure any excess water has evaporated. Pass through a ricer or mash until very smooth.

4. Measure 230 g (8 oz/1 cup) of mashed potato into a large mixing bowl and set aside to cool to room temperature.

5. While the potatoes are cooling, preheat the oven to 180°C (350°F) and line a 21 x 11 x 6 cm (8¼ x 4¼ x 2½ in) loaf (bar) pan with baking paper.

6. In a medium mixing bowl, whisk together the flour and baking powder.

7. Add the maple syrup to the potato and beat with a wooden spoon until smooth. Add the egg and stir until completely incorporated. Stir in the walnuts, brown sugar and the sultanas with the milk. Add the flour mixture to the potato batter and stir until just combined.

8. Pour the batter into the loaf pan and gently smooth the top with a spatula. Bake for about 1 hour and 10 minutes, until a skewer or toothpick inserted in the centre of the tea cake comes out clean. If the cake is browning too quickly, cover loosely with foil.

9. Cool the cake in the pan for 5 minutes before turning out onto a wire rack.

10. When completely cool, place the tea cake on a serving plate. Slice it thick or thin, according to your preference.

11. Store left-over tea cake in the refrigerator in an airtight container for up to 3 days.

double chocolate potato chip cookies

Sweet, salty, chewy, crunchy – this cookie has it all. Serve with a frothy milkshake or a glass of milk for an old-school classic snack with an up-to-date taste.

Use plain salted crinkle-cut potato chips (crisps).

150 g (5½ oz/1 cup) plain (all-purpose) flour, sifted

1 tablespoon malted milk powder, sifted

½ teaspoon baking powder, sifted

125 g (4½ oz) unsalted butter, softened

95 g (3¼ oz/½ cup) brown sugar

55 g (2 oz/¼ cup) caster (superfine) sugar

1 large egg, at room temperature

1 teaspoon natural vanilla extract

100 g (3½ oz) milk chocolate, chopped into 1 cm (½ in) pieces

100 g (3½ oz) white chocolate, chopped into 1 cm (½ in) pieces

75 g (2¾ oz/1½ cups) roughly crushed crinkle-cut potato chips (crisps)

1. Preheat the oven to 180°C (350°F) and line 2 baking trays with baking paper.

2. In a medium mixing bowl, whisk together the flour, malted milk powder and baking powder.

3. In a large mixing bowl or the bowl of a stand mixer, beat the butter and sugars together until light and fluffy, about 4 minutes. Add the egg and stir until completely incorporated. Add the vanilla and stir until combined. Add the flour mixture to the cookie batter and stir until just combined.

4. Add the milk chocolate and white chocolate pieces and the potato chips to the cookie batter and stir until mixed through. Using a 60 ml (2 oz) cookie dough or ice cream scoop, place 6 balls of dough onto each tray, evenly spaced. Bake until the cookies are golden and still slightly soft, about 14 minutes, rotating and swapping the trays halfway through the cooking time.

5. Leave the cookies on the trays for 5 minutes, then place on a wire rack until cool.

6. Serve these warm or cool, according to your preference.

7. Once cool, store the cookies in an airtight container for up to 5 days.

rosemary lemon shortbread cookies

Irresistible with the freshness of lemon and rosemary, I love the way these cookies just melt in the mouth. It's hard to stop at one. They are also great as classic shortbread cookies if you leave out the rosemary and lemon.

150 g (5½ oz/1 cup) plain (all-purpose) flour

160 g (5½ oz/1 cup) potato starch

½ teaspoon sea salt

250 g (9 oz) unsalted butter, at room temperature, chopped

115 g (4 oz/½ cup) caster (superfine) sugar

2 teaspoons finely chopped fresh rosemary

1½ teaspoons grated lemon zest

1 teaspoon natural vanilla extract

1. Preheat the oven to 180°C (350°F) and line 3 baking trays with baking paper.

2. In a medium mixing bowl, whisk together the flour, potato starch and sea salt.

3. In a large mixing bowl or the bowl of a stand mixer, beat the butter and sugar until light and fluffy, about 4 minutes. Add the rosemary, lemon zest and vanilla and stir until incorporated. Add the flour mixture and stir until just combined.

4. Use your hands to roll tablespoons of the dough into balls, placing 8 on each tray, evenly spaced. With a lightly floured fork, flatten the cookies slightly and create a decorative effect.

5. Bake until the cookies are turning golden on the edges, about 15 minutes, rotating the trays about halfway through the cooking time. Cool the cookies on the baking trays for 5 minutes before removing to a wire rack.

6. These are best served when completely cool.

7. Store the cookies in an airtight container for up to 5 days.

chocolate sweet potato bars

Delicious and full of good things like chocolate, pecans and coconut, these chocolate sweet potato bars have the zing of orange and the warmth of cinnamon for the perfect afternoon snack. Serve with a mug of hot chocolate and, if you're feeling indulgent, a dollop of whipped cream on the side.

Use sweet potatoes.

for the base

150 g (5½ oz/1 cup) plain (all-purpose) flour

115 g (4 oz/½ cup) caster (superfine) sugar

40 g (1½ oz/⅓ cup) unsweetened (Dutch) cocoa powder, sifted

½ teaspoon sea salt

150 g (5½ oz) unsalted butter, melted

½ teaspoon natural vanilla extract

for the topping

1 medium sweet potato, about 380 g (13½ oz)

60 g (2 oz) unsalted butter, melted

1 tablespoon cornflour (cornstarch)

¾ teaspoon ground cinnamon

½ teaspoon natural vanilla extract

½ teaspoon finely grated orange zest

¼ teaspoon sea salt

125 g (4½ oz/⅔ cup) brown sugar

2 large eggs, at room temperature

100 g (3½ oz) dark chocolate (70%), chopped into small pieces

90 g (3 oz/¾ cup) chopped pecans

25 g (1 oz/¼ cup) shredded unsweetened coconut

1. Preheat the oven to 200°C (400°F) and line a baking tray with baking paper.

2. Scrub the sweet potato and pierce it a few times with a skewer. Wrap in foil, place on the baking tray and bake until completely tender, about 60–70 minutes, checking with a skewer. When cool enough to handle, peel the sweet potato and pass it through a ricer or mash well until very smooth.

3. Reduce the oven temperature to 180°C (350°C) and line a 32 x 18 cm (12½ x 7 in) baking pan with baking paper.

4. To make the base, in a medium mixing bowl whisk together the flour, caster sugar, cocoa powder and sea salt. Pour the melted butter and vanilla into the flour mixture and stir until combined. Spread the mixture into the base of the prepared baking pan. Bake until just firm, about 15 minutes. Set aside to cool for 10 minutes while you make the topping.

5. To make the topping, in a small bowl, whisk together the melted butter, cornflour, cinnamon, vanilla, orange zest and sea salt.

6. Measure 250 g (9 oz/1 cup) of mashed sweet potato into a medium mixing bowl. Pour in the butter mixture and stir well.

7. In a separate large mixing bowl or the bowl of a stand mixer, whisk the sugar and eggs together until foamy, about 3 minutes. Add the eggs to the sweet potato mixture and stir until well combined. Stir in the chopped chocolate, pecans and coconut.

8. Spread the topping over the base and smooth with a spatula. Bake until lightly puffed and the centre springs back when gently pressed with your finger, about 35 minutes.

9. Place the baking pan on a wire rack to cool. When cold, remove from the pan and cut into bars.

10. Store in an airtight container in the refrigerator for up to 3 days.

coffee dark chocolate potato chip cookies

Everyone who tries these raves about them, without realising the secret ingredient is potato chips. Of course, the dark chocolate and coffee don't hurt, either! These are decadent and a little bit naughty, and needless to say they are on high rotation in my cookie jar.

Use plain salted crinkle-cut potato chips (crisps).

150 g (5½ oz/1 cup) plain (all-purpose) flour, sifted

1 teaspoon instant coffee powder, sifted

½ teaspoon baking powder, sifted

125 g (4½ oz) unsalted butter, softened

95 g (3¼ oz/½ cup) brown sugar

55 g (2 oz/¼ cup) caster (superfine) sugar

1 large egg, at room temperature

1 teaspoon natural vanilla extract

200 g (7 oz) dark chocolate (70%), chopped into 1 cm (½ in) pieces

125 g (4½ oz/1 cup) chopped pecans

50 g (1¾ oz/1 cup) roughly crushed crinkle-cut potato chips (crisps)

1. Preheat the oven to 180°C (350°F) and line 2 baking trays with baking paper.

2. In a medium mixing bowl, whisk together the flour, coffee powder and baking powder.

3. In a large mixing bowl or the bowl of a stand mixer, beat the butter and sugars together until light and fluffy, about 4 minutes. Add the egg and stir until completely incorporated. Add the vanilla and stir until combined. Add the flour mixture to the cookie batter and stir until just combined.

4. Add the chocolate, pecans and potato chips to the cookie batter and stir until mixed through. Using a 60 ml (2 fl oz) cookie dough or ice cream scoop, place 6 balls of dough onto each tray, evenly spaced. Bake until the cookies are golden and still slightly soft, about 14 minutes, rotating and swapping the trays halfway through the cooking time.

5. Leave the cookies on the trays for 5 minutes, then place on a wire rack until cool.

6. Serve these warm or cool, according to your preference.

7. Store the cookies in an airtight container for up to 5 days.

chocolate, sweet potato and chilli raspberry brownie

Sweet potato seriously increases the fudge factor in these brownies, while the cayenne pepper in the raspberries adds a subtle bite that's particularly good. Have these after dinner as a grown up treat. If you prefer, omit the cayenne pepper.

Use orange sweet potatoes.

for the chilli raspberries

180 g (6½ oz/1½ cups) frozen raspberries (no need to thaw first)

1 tablespoon maple syrup

½ teaspoon balsamic vinegar

½ teaspoon cayenne pepper, or to taste

for the brownie batter

1 medium sweet potato, about 260 g (9 oz)

200 g (7 oz) dark chocolate (70%), chopped or broken into pieces

125 g (4½ oz) unsalted butter, chopped

150 g (5½ oz/1 cup) plain (all-purpose) flour, sifted

40 g (1½ oz/⅓ cup) unsweetened (Dutch) cocoa powder, sifted, plus extra to serve

1 teaspoon instant coffee powder, sifted

½ teaspoon baking powder

½ teaspoon sea salt

185 g (6½ oz/1 cup) brown sugar

3 large eggs, at room temperature

1. Preheat the oven to 200°C (400°F).

2. Mix the raspberries, maple syrup, vinegar and cayenne pepper in a medium glass or ceramic baking dish, about 18 x 13 x 5 cm (7 x 5 x 2 in). Roast for 30 minutes, removing from the oven every 10 minutes to stir and squash the berries with the back of a spoon. Set aside to cool. (The raspberries will thicken on standing.)

3. Meanwhile, scrub the sweet potato and pierce a few times with a skewer. Wrap in foil, place on a baking tray and bake until completely tender, about 60–70 minutes, checking with a skewer. When cool enough to handle, peel the sweet potato and pass through a ricer or mash well until very smooth. Set aside to cool to room temperature.

4. Reduce the oven temperature to 170°C (340°F) and line a 20 x 20 x 8 cm (8 x 8 x 3¼ in) baking pan with baking paper.

5. Melt the chocolate and butter in a heatproof bowl placed on top of a saucepan containing about 2 cm (¾ in) of hot water over medium–low heat. Remove the bowl and place it on a tea towel (dish towel) on a work surface, taking care as the bowl may be hot. Stir until the melted chocolate is smooth and glossy. Set aside to cool slightly.

6. In a large mixing bowl, whisk together the flour, cocoa powder, coffee, baking powder and sea salt.

7. In a separate large mixing bowl or the bowl of a stand mixer, whisk the sugar and eggs together until light and foamy, about 3 minutes. Add the chocolate and stir until combined and no streaks of chocolate remain. Measure 185 g (7 oz/¾ cup) of sweet potato and add it to the brownie batter, stirring until well combined. Add the flour mixture and stir until just combined.

8. Tip half of the batter into the prepared baking pan and spread to the edges of the pan. Gently spread the raspberries over the brownie batter with the back of a spoon. Cover the raspberries with the remaining batter. Bake until the brownie is set but still fudgy, about 30 minutes. Pierce the centre of the brownie with a skewer to check if cooked, looking for moist crumbs on the end of the skewer but no liquid.

9. Cool the brownie in the pan before removing. (You can hasten this process by putting the brownie in the refrigerator.) Dust with 2 teaspoons of sifted cocoa powder and cut into 16 squares, to serve.

10. Store the left-over brownie in the refrigerator in an airtight container for up to 3 days.

roasted raspberry and potato frangipane slice

This is always a popular slice when I make it, with the potato giving the topping a deliciously moist texture that complements the almond meal. You could easily replace the roasted raspberries with a good raspberry jam if you wish.

Use floury (starchy or roasting) potatoes; see pages 002–003 for a list of varieties.

for the roasted raspberries

180 g (6½ oz/1½ cups) frozen raspberries (no need to thaw first)

1 tablespoon maple syrup

½ teaspoon balsamic vinegar

for the base

125 g (4½ oz) unsalted butter, softened

55 g (2 oz/¼ cup) caster (superfine) sugar

150 g (5½ oz/1 cup) plain (all-purpose) flour

for the topping

1 medium potato, about 175 g (6 oz), peeled and cut into 2 cm (¾ in) pieces

155 g (5½ oz/1½ cups) almond meal (ground alomonds)

1 teaspoon grated lemon zest

¼ teaspoon sea salt

125 g (4½ oz) unsalted butter, softened

125 g (4½ oz) cream cheese (full-fat), at room temperature

115 g (4 oz/½ cup) caster (superfine) sugar

2 large eggs, at room temperature

25 g (1 oz/¼ cup) flaked almonds

1. Preheat the oven to 200°C (400°F).

2. Mix the raspberries, maple syrup and balsamic vinegar in a medium glass or ceramic baking dish, about 18 x 13 x 5 cm (7 x 5 x 2 in). Roast for 30 minutes, removing from the oven every 10 minutes to stir and squash the berries with the back of a spoon. Set aside to cool. (The raspberries will thicken on standing.)

3. Meanwhile, put the potato in a small saucepan and cover with cold water. Bring to the boil over medium–high heat and boil until very tender, about 12 minutes, testing with the point of a sharp knife. Drain the potato and return them to the saucepan over low heat for 1 minute to ensure any excess water has evaporated. Pass through a ricer or mash well until very smooth.

4. Measure 115 g (4 oz/½ cup) of the mashed potato into a small bowl and set aside to cool.

5. Reduce the oven temperature to 180°C (350°F) and line a 32 x 18 cm (12½ x 7 in) baking pan with baking paper.

6. To make the base, beat the butter and sugar together until the mixture is smooth and fluffy, about 3 minutes. Add the flour and stir until just combined. Spread the mixture into the base of the prepared baking pan (it will be a thin layer). Bake until just starting to look a little golden, about 10–12 minutes. Set aside to cool.

7. Reduce the oven temperature to 150°C (300°F).

8. For the topping, in a small mixing bowl, combine the ground almonds, lemon zest and sea salt.

9. In a large mixing bowl or the bowl of a stand mixer, beat the butter, cream cheese and sugar until fluffy, about 3 minutes. Beat in the eggs, one at a time, making sure the first egg is well incorporated before adding the second egg. Add the mashed potato and stir until no streaks of potato remain in the batter. Add the ground almond mixture and stir until incorporated.

10. Spread the roasted raspberries over the cooled base. Drop spoonfuls of the batter over the raspberries, spreading lightly to cover. Sprinkle the flaked almonds over the topping and press down gently. Bake until the slice looks golden and the centre springs back when lightly pressed with your finger, about 1 hour.

11. Place the baking pan on a wire rack until completely cool.

12. To serve, cut the slice into 16 squares and place on a serving dish.

13. Store the left-over slice in the refrigerator in an airtight container for up to 3 days.

note

I've made these recipes using the Australian measurements, such as 20 ml tablespoons and 250 ml cups. If this is different from your usual measurements, there's a list of conversions below to help you work it out.

In some recipes I've asked you to measure out the exact quantity of potato or sweet potato required. This may mean you'll have some leftovers. But don't throw them away; I like to use any leftovers as a topping on toast or sandwiches. They're really delicious sprinkled with salt and pepper and adorned with whatever other fillings you can find in the refrigerator (and always cheese).

I use a fan-forced oven for my recipes, so if you're using a conventional oven you'll need to increase the temperature by roughly 10–20°C (50–68°F). Cooking times are a guide only. A list of temperature conversions is available on page 160.

measurement conversions

grams	ounces											
5 g	¼ oz	130 g	4½ oz	270 g	9½ oz	420 g	15 oz	570 g	1 lb 4 oz	720 g	1 lb 9 oz
10 g	¼ oz	140 g	5 oz	280 g	10 oz	430 g	15 oz	580 g	1 lb 4 oz	730 g	1 lb 10 oz
20 g	¾ oz	150 g	5½ oz	290 g	10 oz	440 g	15½ oz	590 g	1 lb 5 oz	740 g	1 lb 10 oz
30 g	1 oz	160 g	5½ oz	300 g	10½ oz	450 g	1 lb	600 g	1 lb 5 oz	750 g	1 lb 11 oz
40 g	1½ oz	170 g	6 oz	310 g	11 oz	460 g	1 lb	610 g	1 lb 6 oz	760 g	1 lb 11 oz
50 g	1¾4 oz	180 g	6½ oz	320 g	11½ oz	470 g	1 lb 1 oz	620 g	1 lb 6 oz	770 g	1 lb 11 oz
60 g	2 oz	190 g	6½ oz	330 g	11½ oz	480 g	1 lb 1 oz	630 g	1 lb 6 oz	780 g	1 lb 12 oz
70 g	2½ oz	195 g	7 oz	340 g	12 oz	490 g	1 lb 1 oz	640 g	1 lb 7 oz	790 g	1 lb 12 oz
80 g	2¾ oz	200 g	7 oz	350 g	12½ oz	500 g	1 lb 2 oz	650 g	1 lb 7 oz	800 g	1 lb 12 oz
90 g	3 oz	210 g	7½ oz	360 g	12½ oz	510 g	1 lb 2 oz	660 g	1 lb 7 oz	810 g	1 lb 13 oz
100 g	3½ oz	220 g	8 oz	370 g	13 oz	520 g	1 lb 2 oz	670 g	1½ lb	820 g	1 lb 13 oz
110 g	4 oz	230 g	8 oz	380 g	13½ oz	530 g	1 lb 3 oz	680 g	1½ lb	830 g	1 lb 13 oz
120 g	4½ oz	240 g	8½ oz	390 g	14 oz	540 g	1 lb 3 oz	690 g	1½ lb	840 g	1 lb 14 oz
125 g	4½ oz	250 g	9 oz	400 g	14 oz	550 g	1 lb 3 oz	700 g	1 lb 9 oz	850 g	1 lb 14 oz
		260 g	9 oz	410 g	14½ oz	560 g	1 lb 4 oz	710 g	1 lb 9 oz	860 g	1 lb 14 oz

870 g	1 lb 15 oz	930 g	2 lb 1 oz	990 g	2 lb 3 oz	2.25 kg	5 lb
880 g	1 lb 15 oz	940 g	2 lb 1 oz	1 kg	2 lb 3 oz	2.5 kg	5½ lb
890 g	1 lb 15 oz	950 g	2 lb 2 oz	1.25 kg	2 lb 12 oz	2.75 kg	6 lb
900 g	2 lb	960 g	2 lb 2 oz	1.5 kg	3 lb 5 oz	3 kg	6 lb 10 oz
910 g	2 lb	970 g	2 lb 2 oz	1.75 kg	3 lb 14 oz	3.5 kg	7 lb 12 oz
920 g	2 lb	980 g	2 lb 3 oz	2 kg	4 lb 6 oz	4 kg	8 lb 13 oz

volumes

millilitres	fluid ounces	cups	millilitres	fluid ounces	cups	millilitres	fluid ounces	cups
5 ml	¼ fl oz		160 ml	5½ fl oz		350 ml	12 fl oz	
10 ml	¼ fl oz		170 ml	5½ fl oz	⅔ cup	360 ml	12 fl oz	
15 ml	½ fl oz		180 ml	6 fl oz		370 ml	12½ fl oz	
20 ml	¾ fl oz		190 ml	6 ½ fl oz	¾ cup	375 ml	12½ fl oz	1½ cups
30 ml	1 fl oz		200 ml	7 fl oz		380 ml	13 fl oz	
40 ml	1¼ fl oz		210 ml	7 fl oz		390 ml	13 fl oz	
50 ml	1¾ fl oz		220 ml	7½ fl oz		400 ml	13½ fl oz	
60 ml	2 fl oz	¼ cup	230 ml	8 fl oz		405 ml	13½ fl oz	1 2/3 cups
70 ml	2¼ fl oz		240 ml	8 fl oz		410 ml	14 fl oz	
80 ml	2½ fl oz	⅓ cup	250 ml	8 ½ fl oz	1 cup	420 ml	14 fl oz	
90 ml	3 fl oz		260 ml	9 fl oz		430 ml	14½ fl oz	
100 ml	3½ fl oz		270 ml	9 fl oz		435 ml	15 fl oz	1¾ cups
110 ml	4 fl oz		280 ml	9½ fl oz		440 ml	15 fl oz	
120 ml	4 fl oz		290 ml	10 fl oz		450 ml	15 fl oz	
125 ml	4 fl oz	½ cup	300 ml	10 fl oz		460 ml	15½ fl oz	
130 ml	4½ fl oz		310 ml	10½ fl oz	1¼ cups	470 ml	16 fl oz	
140 ml	4½ fl oz		320 ml	11 fl oz		480 ml	16 fl oz	
150 ml	5 fl oz		330 ml	11 fl oz		490 ml	16½ fl oz	
			340 ml	11½ fl oz	1⅓ cups	500 ml	17 fl oz	2 cups

ml	fl oz	cups	ml	fl oz
510 ml	17 fl oz		710 ml	24 fl oz
520 ml	17½ fl oz		720 ml	24½ fl oz
530 ml	18 fl oz		730 ml	24½ fl oz
540 ml	18 fl oz		740 ml	25 fl oz
550 ml	18½ fl oz		750 ml	25½ fl oz
560 ml	19 fl oz	2¼ cups	760 ml	25½ fl oz
570 ml	19½ fl oz		770 ml	26 fl oz
580 ml	19½ fl oz		780 ml	26½ fl oz
590 ml	20 fl oz		790 ml	26½ fl oz
600 ml	20½ fl oz		800 ml	27 fl oz
610 ml	20½ fl oz		810 ml	27½ fl oz
620 ml	21 fl oz		820 ml	27½ fl oz
625 ml	21 fl oz	2½ cups	830 ml	28 fl oz
630 ml	21½ fl oz		840 ml	28½ fl oz
640 ml	21½ fl oz		850 ml	28½ fl oz
650 ml	22 fl oz		860 ml	29 fl oz
660 ml	22½ fl oz		870 ml	29½ fl oz
670 ml	22½ fl oz		875 ml	29½ fl oz
680 ml	23 fl oz		880 ml	29½ fl oz
685 ml	23 fl oz	2¾ cups	890 ml	30 fl oz
690 ml	23½ fl oz		900 ml	30½ fl oz
700 ml	23½ fl oz		910 ml	30½ fl oz

cups	ml	fl oz	cups
	920 ml	31 fl oz	
	930 ml	31½ fl oz	
	935 ml	31½ fl oz	3¾ cups
	940 ml	32 fl oz	
3 cups	950 ml	32 fl oz	
	960 ml	32½ fl oz	
	970 ml	33 fl oz	
	980 ml	33 fl oz	
	995 ml	33½ fl oz	
	1 litre	34 fl oz	4 cups
3¼ cups	1.25 litres	42 fl oz	5 cups
	1.5 litres	51 fl oz	6 cups
	1.75 litres	60 fl oz	7 cups
	2 litres	68 fl oz	8 cups
	2.25 litres	76 fl oz	9 cups
	2.5 litres	85 fl oz	10 cups
	2.75 litres	93 fl oz	11 cups
3½ cups	3 litres	101 fl oz	12 cups
	3.5 litres	118 fl oz	14 cups
	4 litres	135 fl oz	16 cups

oven temperatures

celsius°	140	150	160	170	180	190	200	210	220
fahrenheit°	275	300	320	340	350	375	400	410	430

index

about the author

Dale Whybrow has loved cooking since receiving her first cookbook at age six, and her family and friends have been stealing her recipes for almost as long (including the one for potato chowder, which won her first prize in a magazine cooking competition). When she's not creating delicious food, Dale works as an educator. She lives in the beautiful city of Sydney, Australia.

acknowledge

Many people played a role in bringing *The Potato Cookbook* to life. The first big thank you is to my daughter, Lauren, who provided the inspiration for this book about one of her most loved foods and also contributed her expertise.

To all at Hardie Grant, in particular Melissa Kayser, and to editor Susie Ashworth, thanks for your guidance.

Thank you to my kitchen crew on the photo shoot, who worked hard to bring the recipes to life and made it a fun week: my friend Lee, my brother John and my mother Dawn – you are amazing. Thanks also to photographer Ben Cole and stylist Gemma Lush for making the food look fabulous.

A big thank you to my wonderful family – Chris, Matt, Tom and Lauren – who ate and ate potatoes (and did the washing up).

And thanks to you, potato lovers, for your enthusiasm for the humble spud.

Published in 2017 by Hardie Grant Books, an imprint of
Hardie Grant Publishing

Hardie Grant Books (Melbourne)
Building 1, 658 Church Street
Richmond, Victoria 3121
hardiegrantbooks.com.au

Hardie Grant Books (London)
5th & 6th Floors
52–54 Southwark Street
London SE1 1UN
hardiegrantbooks.co.uk

A Cataloguing-in-Publication entry is available from
the catalogue of the National Library of Australia at
www.nla.gov.au

The Potato Cookbook
ISBN 9781741175196

Publisher: Melissa Kayser
Commissioning Editor Lauren Whybrow
Managing Editor Marg Bowman
Editors Susie Ashworth & Ariana Klepac
Design Manager Mark Campbell
Designer Vaughan Mossop
Photographer Ben Cole
Stylist Gemma Lush
Production Manager Todd Rechner
Typesetter Megan Ellis

Colour reproduction by Splitting Image Colour Studio
Printed in China by 1010 Printing International Limited